A

SERIOUS CALL

to a

Devout and Holy Life

by

WILLIAM LAW

Edited and Abridged
for the Modern Reader

by

JOHN W. MEISTER and OTHERS

With a Foreword

by

D. ELTON TRUEBLOOD

Westminster John Knox Press
Louisville, Kentucky

Library of Congress Catalog Card No.: 55–5330

PRINTED IN THE UNITED STATES OF AMERICA

12 13 14 15 16 17 18

N O HISTORY of devotional literature can be complete without some reference to William Law. This mild and literary Englishman of the eighteenth century wrote about the life of devotion so lucidly and so pointedly that he cannot be rightly neglected even by a generation of men and women who live in a condition that appears to be very different from his own. Because Law stated so honestly the elements of the human situation, and because that situation has not changed, he can speak directly to sincere seekers of the twentieth century. He dealt with matters that are not altered in the least by modes of travel or systems of human government or standards of living.

William Law, as a young man, gave every promise of a successful career in either the university or the church or both. Born in 1686, in the family of a prosperous businessman in King's Cliffe, Northamptonshire, he entered Emmanuel College, Cambridge in 1705 and became fellow of Emmanuel in 1711. His entire life was altered and his career checked when, in 1714, at the age of twenty-eight, he made a decision that seemed to him a matter of honor. When, on the death of Queen Anne, the Hanoverian prince ascended the throne as George I, holders of academic and ecclesiastical offices were required to swear allegiance to the new monarch, but a minority, including

5

William Law, refused to do so. Because the act that he refused included the abjuration oath, denying the claims of the exiled Stuarts, Law was known henceforth as a nonjuror. In consequence of this act of conscience the young scholar lost his fellowship in Emmanuel College, and also his chance to go forward in the priesthood of the Church of England. He understood the seriousness of his act in apparently ruining his career, but he took the step courageously because he thought the alternative was worse. No defense, he believed, could be given for people " swearing the direct contrary to what they believe." Many who objected equally strongly to the succession decided to conform for the sake of expedience, but Law was made of sterner stuff.

Deprived of his expected career, Law was able to give the greater part of his life to writing and thus made a more permanent contribution than could have been expected without the crisis occasioned by his refusal to swear. After giving up his fellowship at Cambridge his life consisted chiefly of two rather long chapters, during the first of which he was a resident in the Gibbon family, spending some years as tutor of the father of the famous historian.

The other and final chapter was spent with two congenial women companions in the house inherited from his father. Life in this house was devoted to true piety, to charity, and to the education of the young. Once a stranger, without revealing his identity, gave Law an envelope containing one thousand pounds, and Law immediately sent it to his home town to be used in the establishment of a school for fourteen poor children.

Though William Law wrote many books, several of which were highly controversial and of temporary significance, he established the basis of a permanent reputation by the publication, in 1728, of *A Serious Call to a Devout and Holy Life*. This book has been published many times and is usually included in select lists of the classics of Christian devotion. It may fairly be said to be in a class with Jeremy Taylor's *Holy Dying* and Richard Baxter's *Autobiography*. It stands alone in eighteenth century English devotional literature on a par with the great and numerous classics of the seventeenth century.

The great devotional writer lived and thought in marked contrast to the characteristic men of his age. The religious vigor of the Cromwellian period was so far in the past as to be almost forgotten and the standard reaction to religious commitment was one of tolerance or even amusement. Walpole and Bolingbroke seemed to vie with one another, both in their public profession of Christian orthodoxy and in their private derision of it. Religion was supposed to be good for the masses, but any genuine conviction was beneath the dignity of a cultivated gentleman.

The controlling purpose of the life of William Law was the challenge to his unbelieving age, both in thought and practice. Because his generation was in decay he was not satisfied merely to save his own soul. He believed that a redemptive process could be set in motion by the voluntary establishment of what we today should call committed fellowships and he established such a fellowship which lasted from 1740 until his death in 1761. He encouraged sincere Christians, of both sexes, to unite themselves voluntarily into little disciplined societies, " that some might be relieved by their charities, and all be blessed with their prayers, and benefited by their example." This desire for perfection and the group effort in its direction was, he held, far from superstition and indeed the practicable way of recovery. He knew the defects of his period and he had a plan for practical change based on the infectious nature of the dedicated group.

By the force of his writing, Law exercised a profound influence on many minds, the most notable being that of Samuel Johnson. Johnson became a very devout man, in spite of his general roughness of character, and left at his death some of the finest prayers in any language, but this development might never have occurred apart from the influence of the humble nonjuror. Johnson, while a student at Oxford, read the *Serious Call* and consequently became convinced that it was possible to be a Christian without any loss of intellectual integrity. " I expected," said Johnson, " to find it a dull book (as such books generally are), and perhaps to laugh at it, but I found Law quite an overmatch for me; and this was the first occasion of my thinking in earnest of religion after I became capable of rational inquiry."

Though there have been many reprints of Law's most famous work, the present volume represents something new. In this we find the work of a group of ordinary Chirstians of the twentieth century, most of them laymen, who have been so helped by the *Serious Call* that they have undertaken to present the book in condensed but faithful form for the use of their contemporaries. It is hoped that seekers of our age, who are dissatisfied with inadequate answers and with superficial living may find that the enduring work of two centuries ago may speak to their condition now.

I know the men of Fort Wayne, Indiana, who have done this work and I hail their achievement as remarkable. It is one of the most convincing evidences of the renaissance of lay religion in our troubled but promising time.

ELTON TRUEBLOOD.

Contents

Preface

IN THE AUTUMN of 1951 a certain man in our parish walked into my study with an idea that was destined to transform our church. For several months he had been dwelling in the valley of shadows, and during those months he and I had learned to pray together. Our first lessons were learned in the dark and lonely corridor of the polio ward in a local hospital as he kept vigil outside his daughter's room. While iron lungs were filling our ears with the eerie but life-giving sounds of their mechanical breathing, my friend and I were crying importunately into the ear of God with quite another language. God heard our pleading and the prayers of our countless concerned friends. He blessed the skillful efforts of the corps of consecrated doctors and nurses. And at last the day arrived when Kate would return to her home to begin the long years of convalescence.

It was then that my friend began to visit me in my study almost daily, and virtually every visit included a time of prayer. As I recall it, our prayers never were selfish petitions — even in the hospital corridor. But now that we were free of the shadows and sounds of the polio ward we began to discover new dimensions in the world of prayer. There was a reaching-out quality in our prayers which led us to envelop human concerns as the concentric circles emanating from a pebble dropped into a pool gradually envelop the whole pool. There was a reaching-up quality which led us simply to thank God for God. And there was a reaching-down quality which led us to a new sense of at-one-ness with the eternal as we realized that we live and move and have our being in him.

With this kind of experience in the background, my friend came that day with his idea. " I have become convinced," he said, " that you and I have found something that many men in our parish need and want. Why can't we agree that at a certain time each week any man who so desires may meet with us for prayer and for a discussion of anything pertaining to the Christian life? "

Needless to say, this was precisely the sort of idea for which I, as his pastor, had been praying. Within minutes we had arrived at certain ideas or principles which have since become a kind of unwritten charter: We would meet during a lunch hour, which meant that most men could come if they truly wanted to; we would give absolute priority to our prayer time, which meant that no other meeting or project would take precedence over this one; we would make no attempt to attract large numbers of men, which meant that we would heartily welcome anyone who chose to attend out of a felt need; we would appoint no leaders or officers, which meant that we would proceed as the Holy Spirit guided us; and we would select a devotional classic to serve as a basis for our discussion, which meant that we would be lifted above our own limited experiences.

The following Wednesday noon five of us met around a table in the church kitchen. After several devotional classics had been reviewed we agreed to use William Law's A SERIOUS CALL TO A DEVOUT AND HOLY LIFE as the basis for our thinking and praying. We selected this book for the not too admirable reason that none of us had previously read it! Each of us purchased a copy of A SERIOUS CALL and read in it at his leisure. When we came together as a group, one man would read aloud until someone interrupted him with a comment. Some days we read an entire chapter without interruption and other days we read only a sentence or two.

Our first responses to A SERIOUS CALL were not too friendly — certainly not enthusiastic. We felt that Law used too many words to say the obvious. Sometimes he seemed to speak from another world and beside the point of our interests. Sometimes his choice of words and almost always his punctuation stood in the way of our understanding.

But whenever someone suggested that we lay aside A SERIOUS CALL and select another book, there was someone else who offered good reason why we should see this book through to the end. As the weeks passed into months and as our group grew larger, we came to feel that William Law was one of our number. He seemed to speak directly to *us!* For anyone to suggest now that we change books would be tantamount to betraying a faithful friend.

Then one day we reached Chapter 18, in which we read of Paternus and his instruction to his son. Surely here were paragraphs that not only applied to each one of us but that every man in our parish would appreciate reading. At that point, one of the men around the table suggested that we lift out the words spoken by Paternus to his son, mimeograph them, and distribute them among our fellow parishioners. We all thought that a good idea, but someone then remembered other paragraphs that he was certain would be generally appreciated. We soon discovered that each man recalled particular sections as being especially worth-while. And before that session had closed we had decided to abridge the entire book!

We developed this procedure: (1) Each chapter was abridged by one man working independently: (2) the entire group reviewed and amended each abridgment; (3) I then took the results of this group effort and co-ordinated them into the unit as it now stands. In abridging the original work, we eliminated large sections of the text, of course; and we greatly reduced William Law's punctuation, especially commas. For the most part we retained his choice of words. However, we have in a few instances substituted synonyms where the meaning attached to the original has become antiquated.

As I have already indicated, when we began our project we entertained no thought of publishing the abridgment. We thought the effort would be good spiritual discipline for ourselves and we intended only to circulate the product of our labor among our friends and fellow parishioners. It happens, however, that D. Elton Trueblood, the eminent Quaker, is intimately acquainted with our church. Many of our laymen have responded to his vigorous leadership of the Yoke Movement. When he heard of our project and saw some of the chapters we had prepared, he urged us to publish the abridgment. It was his feeling that this shorter and fresher form would bring A Serious Call to the attention of many persons who would otherwise pass it by. He also felt that the abridgment would be used as text or resource material in many college classrooms. We desire to thank Dr. Trueblood for the inspiration that he gave us and for his willingness to write a Foreword interpreting William Law.

At the outset of this preface I mentioned that the idea that ultimately gave rise to this book has also transformed our church. The prayer cell that has produced this abridgment has included wholesale grocers, factory workers, physicians, lawyers, and salesmen. Whenever a group such as this meets weekly for silence, prayer, and serious discussion of the Scriptures or some other devotional classic, a new and transforming power begins to flow into the life of the local church. One of the first evidences of this new power appeared when other people formed themselves into similar cells. We have since enjoyed groups of mothers, of business and professional women, of unmarried adults, of recently married couples, and of choir members.

As the outline of our procedure implies, I must bear the responsibility for any errors of judgment and for any other shortcomings in the abridgment as it now appears. This responsibility I happily bear. On the other hand, any virtues and any unusual wisdom of selectivity that may grace our abridgment are rightly credited to the men who prepared the first draft of each chapter and to the group which rigorously criticized and drastically amended those first drafts.

The men in our prayer cell have asked to remain anonymous, pleading that they are neither professional writers nor authorities in the devotional life. Precisely because they genuinely rate themselves in this humble way, I feel compelled to deny their wish and to introduce them to our readers.

The man who came with the transforming idea is Mr. William T. McKay, a businessman and an elder in our church. The men who prepared the working drafts of the chapters are: George W. McKay, H. Vaughn Scott, M.D., Rev. F. Philip Rice, Earl W. Johns, and Clifford Backstrom. The men who regularly shared the life of our prayer cell during the period of this project, and who contributed much in terms of helpful criticism, are: John E. Culp, M.D., Roy Welty, Rev. Robert Roschy, Howard C. Smith, James Jackson, Robert J. Griffin, and Dale W. McMillen, Jr. All these men save the two ministers are members of our church. Mr. Rice is a colleague on our staff, while Mr. Roschy is a onetime executive secretary of our local council of churches.

We send this book forth in a spirit of humble enthusiasm. We have met a man who has spoken to our condition. We give you what we consider to be the most pertinent of what he has had to say.

CHAPTER I

The Nature and Extent of Christian Devotion

DEVOTION IS neither private nor public prayer, but a life given to God. He is the devout man, therefore, who considers and serves God in everything and who makes all of his life an act of devotion by doing everything in the name of God and under such rules as are conformable to His glory.

We readily acknowledge that God alone is to be the rule and measure of our prayers. We are to pray only in such manner, for such things, and for such ends as are suitable to his glory. Now there is not the least shadow of a reason why we should make God the rule and measure of our prayers but what equally proves it necessary for us to make him the rule and measure of all the other actions of our life. For any way of life, any employment of our time, our talents, or our money, that is not strictly according to the will of God is as great an absurdity and failing as prayers that are not according to the will of God. For there is no other reason why our prayers should be according to the will of God but that we may *live* unto God in the same spirit that we *pray* unto him. Were it not our strict duty to devote all the actions of our lives to God there would be no excellency or wisdom in the most heavenly prayers. Nay, such prayers would be absurdities.

It is for lack of this consistency that we see such confusion in the lives of many people. You see them strict as to times and places of devotion, but when the service of the church is over they are like those who seldom or never attend. In their way of life, in their manner of spending their time or their money, in their cares and fears, in their pleasures and indulgences, in their labor and diversions, they are like the rest of the world. This leads the loose part of the world to make a jest of those who are devout — not because they are really devoted to God, but because they see their devotion goes no farther than their prayers.

Indeed, nothing more absurd can be imagined than wise, sublime, and heavenly prayers added to a life where neither labor nor diversions, neither time nor money, are under the direction of the wisdom and desires of our prayers. If we were to see a man appearing to act wholly with regard to God in everything that he did and yet neglecting all prayer — whether public or private — should we not be amazed at such a man? Yet this is as reasonable as for a person to be strict in observing times and places of prayer while letting the rest of his life be disposed of without regard to the will of God. For it is as great an absurdity to suppose holy prayers without a holiness of life suitable to them as to suppose a holy and divine life without prayers.

It is very observable that there is not one command in all the Gospels for public worship. The frequent attendance at it is never so much as mentioned in all the New Testament. On the other hand, our blessed Saviour and his apostles are wholly taken up in doctrines that relate to everyday life. They call us: to differ in every attitude and way of life from the spirit and way of the world; to renounce the world's goods, to fear none of its evils, to reject its joys, and to have no regard for its happiness; to be as newborn babes who are born into a new state of things; to live as pilgrims in spiritual watching, in holy fear, and in heavenly aspiring after another life; to take up our daily cross, to deny ourselves, to profess the blessedness of mourning, to seek the blessedness of poverty of spirit; to forsake the pride and vanity of riches, to be not anxious for the morrow, to live in the profoundest state of humility, to rejoice in worldly sufferings; to reject the lust of the flesh, the lust of the eyes, and the pride of life; to bear injuries, to forgive and bless our enemies, and to love mankind as God loves them; to give up our whole hearts and affections to God, and strive to enter through the strait gate into a life of eternal glory.

Is it not exceedingly strange, therefore, that people should place so much emphasis upon attendance at public worship — concerning which there is not one precept of our Lord's to be found — and yet neglect these common duties of our ordinary life which are commanded in every page of the Gospels?

If contempt for the temporal and concern for the eternal are necessary attitudes for Christians, it is necessary that these attitudes appear in the whole course of their lives. If self-denial be a condition of salvation, all who would be saved must make self-denial a part of their everyday life. If humility be a Christian duty, then the everyday life of a Christian is to be a constant course of humility. If we are to relieve the naked, the sick, and the prisoner, such expression of love must be the constant effort of our lives. If we are to love our enemies, we must make our common life a visible exercise and demonstration of that love. If contentment and thankfulness be duties to God, they are the duties of every day and in every circumstance of our lives. If we are to be wise and holy as the newborn sons of God, we must renounce everything that is foolish and vain in every part of our daily life. If we are to be new creatures in Christ, we must show that we are so by new ways of living in the world. If we are to follow Christ, it must be in the way we spend each day.

Let us consider an instance among the men. Leo has a great deal of good nature, has kept good company, hates everything that is false and base, is generous to his friends. But Leo has concerned himself so little with religion that he hardly knows the difference between a Jew and a Christian.

Eusebius, on the other hand, has had early impressions of religion and buys books of devotion. He can talk about the feasts and fasts of the Church and knows the names of men outstanding in Church history. You never hear him swear or make a loose jest and when he talks of religion he talks of it as a matter of utmost concern.

Here you see that one person has religion enough to be considered a pious Christian and the other is so far from all appearance of religion that he may be fairly reckoned a heathen. Yet if you look into their everyday life you will not find the least difference.

If you consider Leo and Eusebius in this respect you will find them exactly alike — seeking, using, and enjoying all that can be got in this world in the same manner and for the same ends. You will find that riches, pleasures, indulgences, and recognitions are just as much the happiness of Eusebius as they are of Leo. And yet if Christianity has not changed a man's mind and attitude with relation to these things, what can we say that it has done for him? For if the doctrines of Christianity were practiced, they would make a man as different from other people as a civilized man is different from a savage. If the doctrines of Christianity were practiced, it would be as easy a thing to know a Christian by the outward course of his life as it is now difficult to find a person who lives the Christian life.

CHAPTER II

The Importance of Intention

WE MAY NOW reasonably inquire why the lives of even avowed Christians are thus strangely contrary to the principles of Christianity. Before I give a direct answer to this, however, I desire to inquire why swearing is so common a vice among Christians. Why is it that two in three of the men are guilty of so gross and profane a sin as swearing? There is neither ignorance nor human infirmity to plead for it and it is against an express Commandment and the most plain doctrines of our blessed Saviour. Do but find the reason why the generality of men live in this notorious vice and you will have found the reason why the generality even of professed Christians live so contrary to Christianity.

Now the reason for common swearing is this: Men have not so much as the intention to please God in all their actions. Let a man but have so much piety as to intend to please God in all the actions of his life and then he will never swear more. It is for lack of this intention that you see men who profess religion living in swearing and sensuality — that you see clergymen given to pride, covetousness, and worldly enjoyments. It is for lack of this intention that you see women who profess devotion living in all the folly and vanity of dress and wasting their time in idleness and pleasures.

It was this general intention that made the primitive Christians such eminent examples of devotion, that made the goodly fellowship of the saints, and that made all the glorious army of martyrs and confessors. And if you will stop here and ask yourself why you are not so devoted as the primitive Christians, your own heart will tell you that it is neither through ignorance nor inability but purely because you never thoroughly intended it.

Now, who can be reckoned a Christian while lacking this genuine sincere intention? Yet if it generally existed among Christians it would change the whole face of the world. True piety and exemplary holiness would be as common and visible as buying and selling or any trade in life.

Let a clergyman but have this intention and he will converse as if he had been brought up by an apostle. Let a tradesman but have this intention and it will make him a saint in his shop. His everyday business will be a course of wise and reasonable actions, made holy to God, by being done in obedience to His will and pleasure.

Again, let the gentleman of birth and fortune but have this intention and you will see how it will carry him from every appearance of evil to every evidence of devotion and goodness. He does not ask what is allowable and pardonable, but what is commendable and praiseworthy. He will not, therefore, look at the lives of Christians to learn how he ought to spend his estate, but he will look into the Scriptures and make every doctrine, parable, precept, or instruction that relates to rich men a law to himself in the use of his estate. He will deny himself the pleasures and indulgences that his estate could procure because our blessed Saviour saith, " Woe unto you that are rich! for ye have received your consolation " (Luke 6:24).

Let not anyone look upon this as an imaginary description of the Christian life which looks fine in theory but cannot be put into practice. For it is so far from being an imaginary, impracticable form of life that it has been practiced by great numbers of Christians in former ages who were glad to turn their whole estates into a constant course of charity. And it is so far from being impossible now that if we can find any Christians who sincerely intend to please God in all their actions, as the best and happiest thing in the world, whether they be young or old, single or married, men or women, if they have but this intention, it will be impossible for them to do otherwise.

I have chosen to explain this matter by appealing to this intention because it makes the case so plain and because everyone who has a mind may see it in the clearest light — and feel it in the strongest manner — only by looking into his own heart. For it is as easy for every person to know whether he intends to please God in all his actions as for any servant to know his intention toward his master. Everyone also can as easily tell how he spends his money, and whether he considers how to please God in his spending, as he can tell whether his estate be in money or land. Here is no plea left for ignorance of frailty. Everybody is in the light and everybody has power. And no one can fail except he who is not so much a Christian as to intend to please God in the use of his estate.

You see two persons: one is regular in public and private prayer, the other is not. Now the reason for this difference is not that one has the strength and power to observe prayer while the other has not. The reason is that one intends to please God in the duties of devotion and the other has no such intention. Now the case is the same in the right and wrong use of our time and money.

Here, therefore, let us judge ourselves sincerely. Let us not vainly content ourselves with the common disorders of our lives — the vanity of our expenses, the folly of our diversions, the pride of our habits, the idleness of our lives, and the wasting of our time — fancying that these are such imperfections as we fall into through the unavoidable weakness and frailty of our nature. Rather, let us be assured that these disorders of our daily life are owing to this: that we have not so much Christianity as to intend to please God in all the actions of our life, as the best and happiest thing in the world.

This doctrine does not suppose that we have no need of divine grace or that it is in our power to make ourselves perfect. It only supposes that through the lack of a sincere intention to please God in all our actions we fall into such irregularities of life as by the ordinary means of grace we should have power to avoid; and that we have not that perfection which our present state of grace makes us capable of because we do not so much as intend to have it.

CHAPTER III

The Danger of
Not Intending Our Best

ALTHOUGH THE GOODNESS of God and his rich mercies in
Christ Jesus are sufficient assurance to us that he will be
merciful to our unavoidable weaknesses, we have no reason to
expect the same mercy toward those sins which we have not
intended to avoid. For instance, the common swearer who dies
in that guilt seems to have no title to the divine mercy because
he can no more plead excuse than the man who hid his talent
in the earth could plead his lack of strength to keep it out of
the earth.

If this be right reasoning in the case of a common swearer,
why then do we not carry this way of reasoning to its true ex-
tent? You may have made no progress in the most important
Christian virtues — such as humility and charity. Now if your
failure in these duties is purely owing to your lack of intention
to perform them in any true degree, have you not as little to
plead for yourself — are you not as much without excuse — as
the common swearer? Why, therefore, do you not press these
things home upon your conscience?

You may say that all people fall short of the perfection of
the gospel and, therefore, you are content with your failings.
But this is not the point. The question is not, Can gospel per-

fection be fully attained? but, Have you come as near it as a sincere intention and careful diligence can carry you? If you have made as much progress in the Christian life as you can, then you may justly hope that your imperfections will not be laid to your charge. But if your defects are the result of your negligence and lack of sincere intention, then you leave yourself without excuse.

The salvation of our souls is set forth in Scripture as a thing of difficulty, requiring all diligence and to be worked out with fear and trembling. The Christian life is pictured as continuous striving, and many will fail to attain salvation, not because they took no pains or care about it, but because they did not take pains and care enough.

If my religion is only a formal compliance with those modes of worship which are in fashion where I live; if it costs me no pain or trouble; if it puts me under no rules and restraints; if I have no careful thoughts and sober reflections about it — is it not foolish to think that I am striving to enter in at the strait gate? How can it be said that I am working out my salvation with fear and trembling?

Weak and imperfect men shall — notwithstanding their frailties and defects — be received as having pleased God if they have done their utmost to please him. We cannot offer to God the service of angels. We cannot obey him as if we were in a state of perfection. But fallen men can do their best, and this is the perfection that is required of us. If we stop short of this we stop short of the mercy of God under the terms of the gospel. God has there made no promises of mercy to the slothful and negligent. His mercy is offered only to our frail and imperfect but best endeavors to practice all manner of righteousness.

Now this is not intended to make people anxious or discontented in the service of God, but to fill them with a just fear of living in sloth and idleness. It is only to make them as apprehensive of their state, as humble in their opinion of themselves, as earnest after higher degrees of devotion, as fearful of falling short of happiness as was the great apostle St. Paul when he wrote to the Philippians: " Not as though I had already attained, either were already perfect: . . . but this one thing I do, forgetting those things which are behind, and reaching forth unto those things which are before, I press toward the mark for the prize of the high calling of God in Christ Jesus " (Phil. 3:12–14).

The best way for anyone to know how much he ought to aspire after holiness is to consider how much he thinks will make him easy at the hour of death. Now any man who dares be so serious as to put this question to himself will be forced to answer that at death he will wish he had been as perfect as human nature can be. Is not this, therefore, sufficient to make us not only wish for but work for that degree of perfection?

Penitens was a busy, notable, and prosperous tradesman who died in his thirty-fifth year. A little before his death, when the doctors had given him over, some of his neighbors came one evening to see him and he spoke thus to them: " My friends, I see by the grief that appears in your countenances the tender concern you have for me, and I know the thoughts that you have now about me. You think how melancholy a case it is to see so young a man, and in such flourishing business, delivered up to death. And had I visited any of you in my condition, I should have had the same thoughts of you.

" But now, my friends, my thoughts are no more like your thoughts than my condition is like your condition. It is no trouble to me now to think that I am to die young or before I have developed my estate. These things are now sunk into such mere nothings that I have no name little enough to call them by. For in a few days or hours I am to leave this body to be buried in the earth, and then I shall find myself either forever happy in the favor of God or eternally separated from all light and peace. Can any words sufficiently express the littleness of everything else? Is there any dream like the dream of life, which amuses us with the neglect and disregard of these things?

" When we consider death as a tragedy we think of it only as a tragic separation from the enjoyments of this life. We seldom mourn over an old man who dies rich, but we lament the young who are taken away in the progress of their fortune. You yourselves look upon me with pity, not because I am going unprepared to meet the Judge of the quick and the dead, but because I am to leave a prosperous trade while I am in the flower of my life. What folly of the silliest children is as great as this? For what is there miserable or dreadful in death except the consequences of it?

" Our poor friend Lepidus died, you know, as he was dressing himself for a feast. Do you think he now worries that he did not live until that entertainment was over? Feasts, business, pleasures, and enjoyments seem great things to us while we think of nothing else, but as soon as we add death to them they all sink into an equal littleness. And the soul that is separated from the body no more laments the loss of business than the loss of a feast.

" If I am now going into the joys of God, could there be any reason to grieve that this happened to me before I was forty years of age? Could it be a sad thing to go to heaven before I had made a few more bargains or stood a little longer behind a counter? When you are as near death as I am, you will know that all the different states of life — whether of youth or age, riches or poverty, fame or oblivion — signify no more to you than whether you die in a poor or stately apart-ment. What happens after death makes all that goes before completely trivial.

"But, my friends, how surprised I am that I have not always had these thoughts! What a strange thing it is that a little health or the poor business of a shop should keep us so unaware of these great things that are coming upon us so fast! If I now had a thousand worlds I would give them all for one year more that I might present unto God one year of such devotion and good works as I never before so much as intended.

"When you consider that I have lived free from scandal, and in the communion of the Church, you perhaps wonder to see me so full of remorse and self-condemnation at the ap-proach of death. But, alas! What a poor thing it is to have lived only free from murder, theft, and adultery — which is all that I can say of myself. It is true that I have lived in the communion of the Church and generally frequented its wor-ship and service on Sundays when I was neither too idle nor otherwise occupied with my business and pleasures. But my conformity to the public worship has been more a matter of course than any real intention of doing that which the Church requires. Had that not been so, I would have been oftener at church, more devout when there, and more fearful of neglect-ing it.

"But the thing that now surprises me most is this: that I never *intended* to live up to the gospel. This never so much as entered my head or heart. I never once considered whether I was living as the laws of religion direct or whether my way of life was such as would procure me the mercy of God at this hour. What is the reason that I — who have so often talked of the necessity of rules, methods, and diligence in worldly business — have all this while never once thought of any rules, methods, or managements to carry me on in a life of devotion? Had I only my frailties and imperfections to lament at this time I should lie here humbly trusting in the mercies of God. But, alas! How can I call a general disregard and a thorough neglect of all religious improvement a frailty or imperfection when it was in my power to have been as exact and careful and diligent in a course of devotion as in the business of my trade? I could have called in as many helps, have practiced as many rules, and have been taught as many methods of holy living as of thriving in my shop — had I but so intended and desired it."

Penitens was here going on, but his mouth was stopped by a convulsion which never permitted him to speak any more.

CHAPTER IV

The Way to Please God

HAVING in the first chapter shown that devotion does not imply any form of prayer but a certain form of life that is offered to God everywhere and in everything, I shall now show how we are to devote our labor and employment, our time and fortunes, unto God.

As a good Christian should consider every place as holy, so he should look upon every part of his life as a matter of holiness. The profession of a clergyman is a holy profession because it is a ministration in holy things, but worldly business is to be made holy unto the Lord by being done as a service to him and in conformity to his divine will. Things may and must differ in their use, but yet they are all to be used according to the will of God. Men may and must differ in their employments, but yet they must all act for the same ends, as dutiful servants of God, in the right and devout performance of their several callings. As there is but one God and Father of us all, whose glory gives light and life to everything that lives, whose presence fills all places, whose power supports all beings, whose providence rules all events, so everything that lives — whether in heaven or earth — must all with one spirit live wholly to the praise and glory of this one God and Father of them all.

This is the common business of all persons in this world.

Men and women, rich and poor, must, with bishops and priests, walk before God in the same wise and holy spirit, in the same denial of all vain tempers, and in the same discipline and care of their souls — not only because they have all the same rational nature and are servants of the same God, but because they all seek the same holiness to make them fit for the same happiness to which they are called.

Now to make our labor or employment an acceptable service unto God we must carry it on with the same spirit that is required in an act of charity or a work of love. For, if whether we eat or drink, or whatever we do, we must do all to the glory of God; if we are to use this world as if we used it not; if we are to present our bodies a living sacrifice, holy, acceptable to God; if we are to live by faith, and not by sight, and to have our conversation in heaven, then it is necessary that our daily life be made to glorify God by such attitudes as make our prayers acceptable to him.

If a man labors to be rich, and pursues his business that he may achieve fame and glory in the world, he is no longer serving God in his employment. He is serving other masters and has no more title to a reward from God than he who gives alms that he may be seen, or prays that he may be heard, of men. For vain and earthly desires are no more allowable in our employments than in our charity and devotions.

Most of the employments of life are in themselves lawful; and all those that are so may be made a substantial part of our duty to God if we engage in them only so far, and for such ends, as is suitable to beings who are to live *above* the world all the time that they live *in* the world. This is the only measure of our application to any worldly business — let it be *what* it will, *where* it will, it must have no more of our hands, our hearts, or our time than is consistent with a hearty, daily, careful preparation of ourselves for another life.

Now he who does not look at things of this life in this degree of littleness cannot be said either to feel or believe the greatest truths of Chirstianity. For if he thinks anything great or important in human business, can he be said to feel or believe those Scriptures which represent this life, and the greatest things of life, as bubbles, vapors, dreams, and shadows?

A tradesman may justly think that it is agreeable to the will of God for him to sell such things as are innocent and useful in life, such as help both himself and others and enable them to assist those who want to be assisted. But if, instead of this, he trades only with regard to himself, if it be his chief end to grow rich that he may live in fame and indulgence and to be able to retire from business to idleness and luxury, his trade, as to him, loses all its innocency and is so far from being an acceptable service to God that it is only a more plausible course of covetousness, self-love, and ambition.

Calidus has traded above thirty years in the greatest city of the nation, constantly increasing his trade and his fortune. Every hour of the day is with him an hour of business; and though he eats and drinks very heartily, yet every meal seems to be in a hurry, and he would say grace if he had time. Calidus ends every day at the tavern, but has not leisure to be there till near nine o'clock. He is always forced to drink a good hearty glass to drive thoughts of business out of his head and make his spirits drousy enough for sleep. He does business all the time that he is rising and has settled several matters before he can get to his office. His prayers are a short ejaculation or two, which he never misses in stormy, tempestuous weather because he has always something or other at sea.

Calidus will tell you, with great pleasure, that he has been in this hurry for so many years, and that it would have killed him long ago, but that it has been a rule with him to get out of the town every Saturday and make the Sunday a day of quiet and good refreshment in the country. He is now so rich that he would leave off his business and amuse his old age with building and furnishing a fine house in the country, but that he is afraid he should grow melancholy if he were to quit his business. He will tell you, with great gravity, that it is a dangerous thing for a man who has been used to earning money ever to stop. If thoughts of religion happen at any time to steal into his head, Calidus contents himself with thinking that he never was a friend to heretics and infidels, that he has always been civil to the minister of his parish, and that he has very often given something to charity.

Now this way of life is at such a distance from all the doctrine and discipline of Christianity that no one can live in it through ignorance or frailty. Calidus can no more imagine that he is born again of the Spirit; that he is in Christ a new creature; that he lives here as a stranger and a pilgrim, setting his affections on things above and laying up treasures in heaven — he can no more imagine this than he can think that he has been all his life an apostle working miracles and preaching the gospel.

It must also be admitted that the generality of trading people, especially in great cities, are too much like Calidus. You see them all the week buried in business, unable to think of anything else, and then spending the Sunday in idleness and refreshment, in wandering into the country, in such visits and jovial meetings as make it often the worst day of the week. Now they do not live thus because they cannot support themselves with less care and application to business; but they live thus because they want to grow rich in their trades and to maintain their families in some such figure as a reasonable Christian life has no occasion for. Take away but this desire, and then people of all trades will find themselves at leisure to live every day like Christians, to be careful of every duty of the gospel, to live in a visible course of religion, and be every day strict observers both of private and of public prayer.

Now the only way to do this is for people to consider their trade as something that they are obliged to devote to the glory of God, something that they are to do only in such a manner that they may make it a duty to him. Nothing can be right in business that is not under these rules. Proud views and vain desires in our worldly employments are as truly vices and corruptions as hypocrisy in prayer or vanity in alms. He who labors and toils in a calling that he may make a figure in the world and draw the eyes of people upon the splendor of his condition is as far from the humility of a Christian as he who gives alms that he may be seen of men.

If we could so divide ourselves as to be humble in some respects and proud in others, such humility would be of no service to us because God requires us as truly to be humble in all our actions and designs as to be true and honest in all our actions and designs. We indeed sometimes talk as if a man might be humble in some things and proud in others — humble in his dress, but proud of his learning; humble in his person, but proud in his views and designs. But though this may pass in common discourse, where few things are said according to strict truth, it cannot be allowed when we examine the nature of our actions. It is very possible for a man who lives by cheating to be very punctual in paying for what he buys, but then everyone is assured that he does not do so out of any principle of true honesty. If we could suppose that God rejects pride in our prayers and alms, but bears with pride in our dress, our persons, or our estates, it would be the same thing as to suppose that God condemns falsehood in some actions but allows it in others. For pride in one thing differs from pride in another thing as the robbing of one man differs from the robbing of another.

Enough, I hope, has been said to show you the necessity of thus introducing religion into all the actions of your common life, and of living and acting with the same regard to God in all you do as in your prayers and alms.

Chapter V

Requirements of the Privileged

N0 ONE is to live in his employment for such ends as please his own fancy, but is to do all his business in such a manner as to make it a service unto God. Those who have no particular employment, therefore, are so far from being at greater liberty to live to themselves and to spend their time and fortunes as they please that they are under greater obligations of living wholly unto God in all their actions. They are those of whom much will be required because much is given unto them. All ways of holy living and all kinds of virtue lie open to those who are masters of themselves, their time, and their fortune.

It is as much the duty, therefore, of such persons to make a wise use of their liberty, to devote themselves to all kinds of virtue, to aspire after everything that is holy, to endeavor to be eminent in all good works, and to please God in the highest and most perfect manner — it is as much their duty to be thus wise in the conduct of themselves as it is the duty of a slave to be resigned unto God in his state of slavery. For the more you are free from the common necessities of men, the more you are to imitate the higher perfections of angels.

Had you, Serena, been obliged by the necessities of life to wash clothes for your maintenance or to wait upon some mistress who demanded all your labor, it would then be your duty to serve and glorify God by such humility, obedience, and faithfulness, as might adorn that state of life. It would then be recommended to your care to improve that one talent to its greatest height, that when the time came to be rewarded by the great Judge of the quick and the dead you might be received with a " Well done, thou good and faithful servant: . . . enter thou into the joy of thy lord."

But as God has given you five talents, as he has placed you above the necessities of life in the happy liberty of choosing the most exalted ways of virtue, it is now your duty to turn your five talents into five more. It is your duty to consider how your time and leisure and health and fortune may be made so many happy means of purifying your own soul, improving your fellow creatures in the ways of virtue, and carrying you at last to the greatest heights of eternal glory.

Nourish your soul with good works, give it peace in solitude, get it strength in prayer, make it wise with reading, enlighten it by meditation, make it tender with love, sweeten it with psalms and hymns, and comfort it with frequent reflections upon future glory. Keep your soul in the presence of God, and teach it to imitate those guardian angels which, though they attend on human affairs and the lowest of mankind, yet " always behold the face of your Father which is in heaven." This, Serena, is your profession. For as sure as God is one God, so sure it is that he has but one command to all mankind — whether they be bond or free, rich or poor — and that is: to act up to the excellency of that nature which he has given them, to live by reason, to walk in the light of religion, to use everything as wisdom directs, to glorify God in all his gifts, and dedicate every condition of life to his service.

As we have always the same natures and are everywhere the

servants of the same God, as every place is equally full of his presence and everything is equally his gift, so we must always do everything as the servants of God and we must use everything as that ought to be used which belongs to God. If, therefore, some people fancy that they must be grave and solemn at church, but silly at home; that they must live by some rule on a Sunday, but may spend other days by chance; that they must have some times of prayer, but may waste the rest of their time as they please; that they must give some money in charity, but may squander away the rest as they have a mind — such people have not enough considered the nature of religion or the true reasons of piety.

If anyone could show that we need not *always* act as in the divine presence, that we need not consider and use *everything* as the gift of God, and that we need not *always* live by reason — the same arguments would show that we need *never* act as in the presence of God nor need we make religion and reason the measure of *any* of our actions. If, therefore, we are to live unto God at any time or in any place, we are to live unto him at all times and in all places. If we are to use anything as the gift of God, we are to use everything as his gift. If we are to do anything by strict rules of reason, we are to do everything in the same manner.

They, therefore, who confine religion to times and places, and who think that it is being too strict and rigid to make religion give laws to all their actions and ways of living — they who think thus mistake the whole nature of religion. They may well be said to mistake the whole nature of wisdom who do not think it desirable to be always wise. He has not learned the nature of piety who thinks it too much to be pious in all his actions. He does not sufficiently understand what reason is who does not earnestly desire to live in everything according to reason. It is therefore an immutable law of God that all rational things should act reasonably in all their actions. This is a law that is as unchangeable as God and can no more cease to be than God can cease to be a God of wisdom and order. They, therefore, who plead for indulgences and vanities — for the misuse of time or money — plead for a rebellion against our nature, for a rebellion against God.

The infirmities of human life make such food and raiment necessary for us as angels do not need. But it is no more allowable for us to turn these necessities into follies, and indulge ourselves in the luxury of food or the vanities of dress, than it is allowable for angels to act below the dignity of their proper state. Our blessed Saviour has plainly turned our thoughts this way by making this petition a constant part of all our prayers: " Thy will be done in earth, as it is in heaven." Here is plain proof that the obedience of men is to imitate the obedience of angels, and that rational beings on earth are to live unto God as rational beings in heaven live unto him.

When, therefore, you would represent to your mind how Christians ought to live unto God and in what degrees of wisdom and holiness they ought to use the things of this life, you must not look at the world but you must look up to God and the society of angels. You must look to all the highest precepts of the gospel; you must examine yourself by the spirit of Christ; you must think how the wisest men in the world have lived; you must think how departed souls would live if they were again to act the short part of a human life; you must think what degrees of wisdom and holiness you will wish for when you are leaving the world.

Now this is not overstraining the matter or proposing to ourselves any needless perfection. It is but barely complying with the apostle's advice where he says, " Finally, brethren, whatsoever things are true, . . . whatsoever things are just, whatsoever things are pure, . . . whatsoever things are of good report; if there be any virtue, and if there be any praise, think on these things." For no one can come near the doctrine of this passage but he who proposes to himself to do everything in this life as the servant of God, to live by reason in everything that he does, and to make the wisdom and holiness of the gospel the rule and measure of his life.

CHAPTER VI

The Wise Use of Our Estates and Fortunes

A S THE HOLINESS of Christianity consecrates all states and employments of life unto God, requiring us to do and use everything as the servants of God, so are we more specially obliged to observe this religious exactness in the use of our estates and fortunes. The reason for this would appear very plain if we were only to consider that our estates are as much the gift of God as our eyes or our hands. We are no more to bury or throw away our estates at pleasure than we are to put out our eyes or throw away our limbs as we please.

But besides this consideration there are other great and important reasons why we should be religiously exact in the use of our estates. First, because the manner of spending our estates enters so far into the business of every day that our common life must be much of the same nature as our common way of spending our estates. If reason and religion govern us in this, then reason and religion have great hold on us. But if humor, pride, and fancy are the measures of our spending our estates, then humor, pride, and fancy will have the direction of the greatest part of our life.

Secondly, another great reason for devoting all our estates to right uses is this: because it is capable of being used to the most excellent purposes and is so great a means of doing good. If we part with our money in foolish ways, we part with a great power of comforting our fellow creatures and of making ourselves forever blessed. If there be nothing so glorious as doing good, if there be nothing that makes us so like unto God, then nothing can be so glorious in the use of our money as to use it all in works of love and goodness — making ourselves friends and fathers and benefactors to all our fellow creatures, imitating the divine love, and turning all our power into acts of generosity, care, and kindness to such as are in need of it.

Now money has very much the nature of eyes and feet. If we either lock it up in chests or waste it in needless and ridiculous expenses upon ourselves, while the poor and the distressed require it for their necessary wants, we are not far from the cruelty of him who chooses rather to adorn his house with his hands and eyes than to give them to those who need them. If we choose to indulge ourselves in such expensive enjoyments as have no real use in them, such as satisfy no real want, rather than to entitle ourselves to an eternal reward by disposing of our money well, we are guilty of his madness who chooses rather to lock up his eyes and hands than to make himself forever blessed by giving them to those who need them.

Thirdly, if we waste our money we are not only guilty of wasting a talent which God has given us but we do ourselves this further harm: we turn this useful talent into a powerful means of corrupting ourselves. So far as it is spent wrong, so far it is spent in support of some wrong purpose which, as Christians and reasonable men, we are obliged to renounce. If, therefore, you do not spend your money in doing good to others, you must spend it to the hurt of yourself. You will act like a man who would refuse to give a cordial to a sick friend, though he could not drink it himself without inflaming his blood. For this is the case of superfluous money: if you give it to those who need it, it is a cordial; if you spend it upon yourself in something that you do not need, it only inflames and disorders your mind and makes you worse than you would be without it.

Therefore, money thus spent is not merely wasted or lost. It is spent for bad purposes and miserable effects, and makes us less able to live up to the sublime doctrines of the gospel. It is like keeping money from the poor to buy poison for ourselves.

So on all accounts, whether we consider our fortune as a talent and a trust from God, or as the great good that it enables us to do, or as the great harm it does to ourselves if idly spent — on all these great accounts it appears that it is absolutely necessary to make reason and religion the strict rule of using all our fortune.

I shall only produce one remarkable passage of Scripture, which is sufficient to justify all that I have said concerning this religious use of all our fortune:

" When the Son of man shall come in his glory, and all the holy angels with him, then shall he sit upon the throne of his glory: And before him shall be gathered all nations: and he shall separate them one from another, as a shepherd divideth his sheep from the goats: And he shall set the sheep on his right hand, but the goats on the left. Then shall the King say unto them on his right hand, Come, ye blessed of my Father, inherit the kingdom prepared for you from the foundation of the world: For I was ahungered, and ye gave me meat: I was thirsty, and ye gave me drink: I was a stranger, and ye took me in: Naked, and ye clothed me: I was sick, and ye visited me: I was in prison, and ye came unto me. Then shall the righteous answer him, saying, Lord, when saw we thee ahungered, fed thee? or thirsty, and gave thee drink? When saw we thee a stranger, and took thee in? or naked, and clothed thee? Or when saw we thee sick, or in prison, and came unto thee? And the King shall answer and say unto them, Verily I say unto you, Inasmuch as ye have done it unto one of the least of these my brethren, ye have done it unto me. Then shall he say also unto them on the left hand, Depart from me, ye cursed, into everlasting fire, prepared for the devil and his angels: For I was ahungered, and ye gave me no meat: I was thirsty, and ye gave me no drink: I was a stranger, and ye took me not in: naked, and ye clothed me not: sick, and in prison, and ye visited me not. Then shall they also answer him, saying, Lord, when saw we thee ahungered, or athirst, or a stranger, or naked, or sick, or in prison, and did not minister unto thee? Then shall he answer them, saying, Verily I say unto you, Inasmuch as ye did it not to one of the least of these, ye did it not to me. And these shall go away into everlasting punishment: but the righteous into life eternal " (Matt. 25:31–46).

Some people, even of those who may be reckoned virtuous Christians, look upon this text only as a general recommendation of occasional works of charity. It shows, however, the necessity not only of occasional charities now and then, but the necessity of such an entire charitable life as in a continual exercise of all such works of charity we are able to perform.

Now the rule is very plain and easy. Who is the humble, or meek, or devout, or just, or faithful man? Is it he who has several times done acts of humility, meekness, devotion, justice, or fidelity? No. It is he, rather, who lives in the habitual exercise of these virtues. In like manner, he only can be said to have performed these works of charity who lives in the habitual exercise of them to the utmost of his power. He only has performed the duty of divine love who loves God with all his heart, and with all his mind, and with all his strength. And he only has performed the duty of these good works who has done them with all his heart, and with all his mind, and with all his strength. For there is no other measure of our doing good than our power of doing it.

Now the rule of forgiving is also the rule of giving. You are not to give or do good to seven, but to seventy times seven. You are not to cease from giving because you have given often to the same person, or to other persons. Rather, you must look upon yourself as greatly obligated to continue relieving those who continue in need as you were obliged to relieve them once or twice.

And the reason for all this is very plain: there is the same goodness, the same excellency, and the same necessity of being thus charitable at one time as at another. It is as much the best use of our money to be always doing good with it as it is the best use of it at any particular time — so that which is a reason for a charitable action is as good a reason for a charitable life.

That which is a reason for forgiving one offense is the same reason for forgiving all offenses, for such charity has nothing to recommend it today but what will be the same recommendation of it tomorrow. And you cannot neglect it at one time without being guilty of the same sin as if you neglected it at another time. As sure, therefore, as these works of charity are necessary to salvation, so sure is it that we are to do them to the utmost of our power — not today or tomorrow but through the whole course of our life. Either you must so far renounce your Christianity as to say that you need never perform any of these good works or you must own that you are to perform them all your life in as high a degree as you are able. There is no middle way to be taken, any more than there is a middle way between pride and humility or temperance and intemperance.

Chapter VII

The Wrong Use of Our Estates
and Fortunes

I T HAS BEEN OBSERVED that a prudent and religious care is to be used in the manner of spending our money or estate, because according as we are wise or imprudent in this respect the whole course of our lives will be either very wise or very full of folly.

Persons who are well affected to religion, who receive instructions of piety with pleasure and satisfaction, often wonder why they make no greater progress in that religion which they so much admire. Now the reason is this: it is because religion lives only in their head, but something else has possession of their heart. Therefore, they continue from year to year mere admirers and praisers of piety without ever coming up to the reality and perfection of its precepts.

If it be asked why religion does not get possession of their hearts, the reason is this: it is because their hearts are constantly employed, perverted, and kept in a wrong state by the indiscreet use of such things as are lawful to be used. The use and enjoyment of their estate is lawful, and, therefore, it never comes into their heads to imagine any great danger from that quarter. Yet our souls may receive an infinite hurt and be rendered incapable of all virtue merely by the use of innocent and lawful things.

What is more innocent than rest and retirement? And yet what more dangerous than sloth and idleness? What is more lawful than eating and drinking? And yet what more destructive of all virtue — what more fruitful of all vice — than sensuality and indulgence? How lawful and praiseworthy is the care of a family! And yet how certainly are many people rendered incapable of all virtue by a worldly and solicitous attitude toward the family!

Now it is for lack of religious exactness in the use of these innocent and lawful things that religion cannot get possession of our hearts. And it is in the right and prudent management of ourselves as to these things that all the art of holy living chiefly consists.

Gross sins are plainly seen and easily avoided by persons who profess religion. But it is difficult to make people at all sensible to the peril of the indiscreet and dangerous use of innocent and lawful things. These persons, as has been observed, may live free from debaucheries and may be friends of religion so far as to praise and speak well of it, and admire it in their imaginations. But it cannot govern their hearts and be the spirit of their actions till they change their way of life and let religion give laws to the use and spending of their estate.

Flavia and Miranda are two maiden sisters who each have two hundred pounds a year. They buried their parents twenty years ago, and have since that time spent their estate as they pleased.

Flavia has been the wonder of all her friends for her excellent management in making so surprising a figure on so moderate a fortune. Several ladies who have twice her fortune are not able to be always so genteel and so constant at all places of pleasure and expense. Flavia is very orthodox — she talks warmly against heretics and schismatics, is generally at church, and often at the sacrament. She once commended a sermon that was against the pride and vanity of dress, and thought it was against Lucinda, whom she takes to be a great deal finer than she need be.

If anyone asks Flavia to do something in charity, if she likes the person who makes the proposal or happens to be in a right mood, she will toss him a half crown or a crown and tell him if he knew what a long milliner's bill she had just received he would think it a great deal for her to give. A quarter of a year after this she hears a sermon upon the necessity of charity. She thinks that the man preaches well, that it is a very proper subject, and that people need to be put in mind of it. But she applies nothing to herself because she remembers that she gave a crown some time ago when she could so ill spare it.

As for poor people themselves, she will admit of no complaints from them. She is very positive they are all cheats and liars and will say anything to get relief. Therefore, it must be a sin to encourage them in their evil ways. You would think Flavia had the tenderest conscience in the world if you were to see how scrupulous and apprehensive she is of the guilt and danger of giving amiss.

She buys all books of wit and humor, and has made an expensive collection of all our English poets. For, she says, one cannot have a true taste of any of them without being conversant with them all. She will sometimes read a book of piety — if it is a short one, if it is much commended for style and language, and if she knows where to borrow it.

Flavia is very idle and yet fond of fine work. This makes her often sit working in bed until noon, and be told many a long story before she is up. I need not tell you, then, that her morning devotions are not always rightly performed.

Flavia would be a miracle of piety if she were but half so careful of her soul as she is of her body. The rising of a pimple in her face or the sting of a gnat will make her keep to her room two or three days — so that it costs her a great deal in sleeping pills, in spirits for the head, in drops for the nerves, in cordials for the stomach, and in saffron for her tea.

If you visit Flavia on Sunday you will always meet good company and you will know what is doing in the world. Flavia thinks they are atheists who play cards on Sunday, but as soon as she comes from church she will tell you the nicety of all the games, what cards she held, how she played them, and the history of all that happened at play. If you would know how cross Lucius is to his wife, what ill-natured things he says to her when nobody hears him; if you would know how they hate one another in their hearts though they appear so kind in public — you must visit Flavia on Sunday. But still she has so great a regard for the holiness of Sunday that she has turned a poor old widow out of her house for having been once found mending her clothes on Sunday night.

Thus lives Flavia — and if she lives ten years longer she will have spent about fifteen hundred and sixty Sundays after this manner. She will have worn about two hundred different suits of clothes. Out of these thirty years of her life, fifteen will have been disposed of in bed. And about fourteen of the remaining fifteen will have been consumed in eating, drinking, dressing, visiting, conversation, reading and hearing plays and romances, at operas, assemblies, balls, and diversions. For you may reckon thus spent all the time that she is up, except about an hour and a half that is disposed of at church most Sundays in the year.

I shall not take upon me to say that it is impossible for

Flavia to be saved, but this much must be said: she has no grounds from Scripture to think she is in the way of salvation. If you were to hear her say that she had lived all her life like Anna the prophetess, who " departed not from the temple, but served God with fastings and prayers night and day," you would look upon her as very extravagant. Yet this would be no greater extravagance than for her to say that she had been striving to enter in at the strait gate or making any one doctrine of the gospel a rule of her life.

Here it is to be well observed that the vain turn of mind, the irreligion, and the folly of this whole life of Flavia is all owing to the manner of using her estate. It is this that has formed her spirit, that has given life to every idle attitude, that has supported every trifling passion, and that has kept her from all thoughts of a prudent, useful, and devout life.

When her parents died she had no thought about her two hundred pounds a year, except that she had so much money to do with what she would, to spend upon herself, and to purchase the pleasures and gratifications of all her passions. She might have been humble, serious, devout, a lover of good books, an admirer of prayer and retirement, careful of her time, diligent in good works, full of charity and the love of God — but the imprudent use of her estate forced all the contrary attitudes upon her.

Now, though the irregular, trifling spirit of this character belongs, I hope, to but few people, yet many may here learn some instruction from it and perhaps see something of their own spirit in it. For as Flavia seems to be undone by the unreasonable use of her fortune, so the lowness of most people's virtue, the imperfections of their piety, and the disorders of their passions are generally owing to their imprudent use and enjoyment of lawful and innocent things.

More people are kept from a true sense and taste of religion by a regular kind of sensuality and indulgence than by gross drunkenness. More men live without regard for the great duties of piety through too great a concern for worldly goods than through direct injustice. For all these things are only little when they are compared to great sins — and though they are little in that respect, yet they are great as they are impediments and hindrances to the spiritual life.

If we, therefore, would make real progress in religion, we must not only abhor gross and notorious sins, but we must regulate the innocent and lawful parts of our behavior, and put the most common and allowed actions of life under the rules of discretion and piety.

Chapter VIII

Some Effects of the Wise Use
of an Estate

A NY ONE pious regularity of any one part of our life is of
great advantage, not only on its own account, but as it
teaches us to live by rule and to think of the government of ourselves. He who has brought any one part of his life under the
rules of religion may thence be taught to extend the same order
and regularity into other parts of his life. He who once knows
the value and reaps the advantage of a well-ordered time will
not long be a stranger to the value of anything else that is of
any real concern to him.

As the proverb saith, "He that has begun well has half
done." So he who has begun to live by rule has gone a great
way toward the perfection of his life.

By "rule" must here be constantly understood a religious
rule observed upon a principle of duty to God. For if a man
should oblige himself to be moderate in his meals only in regard to his stomach, or abstain from drinking only to avoid the
headache, he might be exact in these rules without being at all
the better man for them. But when he is moderate and regular
in either of these things out of a sense of Christian sobriety and
self-denial, that he may offer unto God a more reasonable and
holy life, then it is that the smallest rule of this kind is naturally
the beginning of great piety.

Now the two things that most need to be under a strict rule — and are the greatest blessings both to ourselves and to others when they are rightly used — are our time and our money. These talents are continual means and opportunities of doing good. He who is strict and exact in the wise management of either of these cannot be long ignorant of the right use of the other. And he who is happy in the religious care and disposal of them both has already ascended several steps up the ladder of Christian perfection.

Miranda, the sister of Flavia, is a sober and reasonable Christian. As soon as she was mistress of her time and fortune it was her first thought how she might best fulfill everything that God required of her in the use of them, and how she might make the best and happiest use of this short life. She depends upon the truth of what our blessed Lord hath said, that there is but "one thing needful," and she makes her whole life one continual labor after it. She has but one reason for doing or not doing, for liking or not liking, anything — and that is the will of God. She is not so weak as to pretend to add what is called the fine lady to the true Christian. Miranda thinks too well to be taken with the sound of such silly words. She has renounced the world to follow Christ in the exercise of humility, charity, devotion, abstinence, and heavenly affections.

Miranda does not divide her duty among God, her neighbor, and herself. Rather, she considers all as due to God and so does everything in his name and for his sake. This makes her consider her fortune as the gift of God, to be used, as is everything that belongs to God, for the wise and reasonable ends of a Christian and holy life. She thinks it the same folly to indulge herself in needless, vain expenses as to give to other people to spend in the same way. If we are angry with a poor man and look upon him as a wretch when he throws away that which should buy his own bread, how must we appear in the sight of God if we make wanton use of that which should buy bread and clothes for the hungry and naked, who are as near and dear to God as we are? This is the spirit of Miranda, and thus she uses the gifts of God. She is only one of a number of poor people who are relieved out of her fortune, and she differs from them only in the blessedness of giving.

Every morning sees her early at her prayers. She rejoices in the beginning of every day, because it begins her rules of holy living and brings the pleasure of repeating them. She seems to be as a guardian angel to those who dwell about her, and God has heard several of her private prayers before the light is suffered to enter into her sister's room.

When you see her at work you see the same wisdom that governs all her other actions. She is doing something that is necessary either for herself or for others. When there is no wisdom to be observed in the employment of her hands, when there is no useful or charitable work to be done, Miranda will work no more.

At her table she lives strictly by this rule of Scripture: " Whether ye eat, or drink, or whatsoever ye do, do all to the glory of God." This makes her begin and end every meal — as she begins and ends every day — with acts of devotion. She eats and drinks only for the sake of living. If Miranda were to run a race for her life she would submit to a diet proper for it. But as the race which is set before her is a race of holiness, purity, and heavenly affection, her everyday diet has only this one end: to make her body fitter for this spiritual race.

The holy Scriptures, especially the New Testament, are her daily study. These she reads with a watchful attention, constantly casting an eye upon herself and testing herself by every doctrine that is there. When she has the New Testament in her hand she supposes herself at the feet of our Saviour and his apostles.

She is sometimes afraid that she lays out too much money in books, because she cannot forbear buying all practical books of any note. Of all human writings the lives of devout persons and eminent saints are her greatest delight. In these she searches as for hidden treasure — hoping to find some secret of holy living which she may make her own. By this means Miranda has her head and her heart so stored with all the principles of wisdom and holiness that if you are in her company you must be made wiser and better.

To relate her charity would be to relate the history of every day for twenty years. She has set up near twenty poor tradesmen who had failed in their business, and saved as many from failing. She has educated several poor children and put them in an honest employment. As soon as a laborer is confined at home with sickness she sends him, till he recovers, twice the value of his wages, that he may have one part to give to his family as usual and the other to provide things convenient for his sickness.

If there is any poor man or woman who is more than ordinarily wicked Miranda has her eye upon him. She watches his time of need and adversity, and if she can discover that he is in any great affliction she gives him speedy relief. There is nothing in the character of Miranda more to be admired than this trait. For this tenderness of affection toward the most abandoned sinners is the highest instance of a divine and God-like soul.

Miranda never lacks compassion, even to common beggars —

especially toward those who are old or sick, or full of sores, or who want eyes or limbs. If a poor old traveler tells her that he has neither strength nor food nor money left, she never tells him that she cannot relieve him because he may be a cheat or because she does not know him. But she relieves him because he *is* a stranger and unknown to her. Miranda considers that our blessed Saviour and his apostles were kind to beggars — that they spoke comfortably to them, healed their diseases, and restored eyes and limbs to the lame and the blind. Miranda, therefore, never treats beggars with disregard and aversion, but she imitates the kindness of our Saviour and his apostles. Though she cannot, like them, work miracles for their relief, yet she relieves them with that power which she has.

"It may be," says Miranda, "that I may often give to those who do not deserve it, or who will make an ill use of my alms. But what then? Is not this the very method of divine goodness? Does not God make his sun to rise on the evil and on the good? Do I not beg of God to deal with me according to his own great goodness rather than according to my merit? Shall I, then, be so absurd as to withhold my charity from a poor brother because he may not deserve it? Shall I use a measure toward him which I pray God never to use toward me?

"You will perhaps say that by this means I encourage people to be beggars. But the same thoughtless objection may be made against all kinds of charities, for they may encourage people to depend upon them. The same may be said against forgiving our enemies, for it may encourage people to do us hurt. The same may be said even against the goodness of God, that by pouring his blessings on the evil and on the good, on the just and on the unjust, evil and unjust men are encouraged in their wicked ways. But when the love of God dwells in you, when it has enlarged your heart and filled you with mercy and compassion, you will make no more such objections as these."

This is the spirit and this is the life of the devout Miranda. If she lives ten years longer she will have spent sixty hundred pounds in charity, for that which she allows herself may fairly be reckoned among her alms.

When she dies she must shine among apostles and saints and martyrs. She must stand among the first servants of God, and be glorious among those who have fought the good fight and finished their course with joy.

Chapter IX

Some Reflections Upon
the Life of Miranda

N OW THIS LIFE of Miranda, which I heartily recommend
for imitation, may seem contrary to the way and fashion
of the world but is founded upon the plainest doctrines of
Christianity. To live as she does is as truly consistent with the
gospel of Christ as to be baptized or to receive the sacrament.
Her spirit is that which animated the saints of former ages —
and it is because they lived as she does that we now celebrate
their memories and praise God for their examples.

There is nothing whimsical, trifling, or unreasonable in her
character, but everything there described is a right and proper
instance of a solid and real piety. It is as easy to show that it
is whimsical to go to church or to say your prayers as to show
that it is whimsical to observe any of these rules of life. For all
of Miranda's rules of living unto God, of spending her time
and fortune, of eating, working, dressing, and conversing, are
as substantial parts of a reasonable and holy life as are devotion and prayer.

Now why is it that when you think of a saint or eminent
servant of God you cannot imagine vanity of apparel? Is it
not because it is inconsistent with such a right state of heart
and such a true and exalted piety? And is not this, therefore,

a demonstration that where such vanity is admitted, there a right state of heart and a true and exalted piety must needs be lacking? For as certainly as the Virgin Mary could not indulge herself or conform to the vanity of the world in dress and figure, so certain is it that none can indulge themselves in this vanity except those who lack her piety. Consequently, it must be acknowledged that all needless and expensive finery of dress is the effect of a self-centered heart — one that is not governed by the true spirit of religion.

Covetousness is not a crime because there is any harm in gold and silver, but because it reveals a foolish and unreasonable state of mind. In like manner, the expensive finery of dress is not a crime because there is anything good or evil in clothes, but because the expensive ornaments of clothing show a foolish and unreasonable state of heart which abuses the purpose of clothing and turns the necessities of life into so many instances of pride and folly.

As in the matter of temperance there is no rule but the sobriety that is according to the doctrines and spirit of our religion, so in the matter of apparel there is no rule but such a right use of clothes as is strictly according to the doctrines and spirit of our religion. To pretend to make the way of the world our measure in these things is as weak and absurd as to make the way of the world the measure of our sobriety, abstinence, or humility. It is a pretense that is exceedingly absurd in the mouths of Christians, who are to be so far from conforming to the fashions of this life that to have overcome the world is made an essential mark of Christianity.

If you would be a good Christian, there is but one way — you must live wholly unto God. You must live according to the wisdom that comes from God. You must act according to right judgments of the nature and value of things. You must live in the exercise of holy and heavenly affections. And you must use all the gifts of God to his praise and glory.

Some persons, perhaps, who admire the purity and perfection of this life of Miranda may say: " How can it be proposed as a general example? How can we who are married, or we who are under the direction of our parents, imitate such a life? "

It is answered, Just as you may imitate the life of our blessed Saviour and his apostles even though the circumstances of our Saviour's life and the state and condition of his apostles were more different from yours than are those of Miranda. Their life, the purity and perfection of their behaviour, is the common example that is proposed to all Christians. It is their spirit, therefore — their piety, their love of God — that you are to imitate and not the particular form of their life.

Act under God as they did. Direct your common actions to that end which they did. Glorify your proper state with such love of God, such love for your neighbor, such humility and self-denial, as they did. And then, though you are only teaching your own children while St. Paul is converting whole nations, yet you are following his steps and acting after his example.

Thus, for instance, if a man should deny himself such use of liquors as is lawful, if he should refrain from such expense in his drink as might be allowed without sin — if he should do this not only for the sake of a more pious self-denial, but that he might be able to relieve and refresh the helpless, poor, and sick — he might be said to do that which was highly suitable to the true spirit, though not absolutely required by the letter, of the law of Christ.

Or, again, if another should abstain from the use of that

which is lawful in dress, if he should be more frugal than the necessities of religion absolutely require — if he should do this not only as a means of a better humility, but that he may be more able to clothe other people — he might he said to do that which was highly suitable to the true spirit, though not absolutely required by the letter, of the law of Christ.

For if those who give a cup of cold water to a disciple of Christ shall not lose their reward, how dear must they be to Christ who often give themselves water that they may be able to give wine to the sick and languishing members of Christ's body!

God may be served and glorified in every state and condition of life. But as there are some states of life more desirable than others — that more purify our natures, that more improve our virtues and dedicate us unto God in a higher manner — so those who are at liberty to choose for themselves seem to be called by God to be more eminently devoted to his service.

Ever since the beginning of Christianity there have been two orders or ranks of people among good Christians. The one feared and served God in the common offices and business of a secular, worldly life. The other — renouncing the common business and such common enjoyments of life as riches, marriage, honors, and pleasures — devoted themselves to voluntary poverty, virginity, devotion, and retirement, that by this means they might live wholly unto God in the daily exercise of divine and heavenly life.

If, therefore, persons of either sex, moved by the life of Miranda and desirous of perfection, should unite themselves into little societies professing voluntary poverty, virginity, retirement, and devotion, living upon bare necessities that others might be relieved by their charities — or if they should practice the same manner of life in as high a degree as they could by themselves — such persons, so far from being chargeable with any superstition or blind devotion, might be justly said to restore the piety that was the boast and glory of the Church when its greatest saints were alive.

If truth itself has assured us that there is but one thing needful, what wonder is it that there should be some among Christians so full of faith as to desire such a separation from the world that their care and attention to the one thing needful may not be interrupted?

If our blessed Lord hath said, " If thou wilt be perfect, go and sell that thou hast, and give to the poor, and thou shalt have treasure in heaven: and come and follow me," what wonder is it that there should be among Christians some such zealous followers of Christ, so intent upon heavenly treasure and so desirous of perfection, that they should renounce the enjoyment of their estates, choose a voluntary poverty, and practice love to the best of their ability?

I have made this little appeal to antiquity and quoted these few passages of Scripture to support some uncommon practices in the life of Miranda. And I have shown that her highest rules of holy living, her devotion, self-denial, and renunciation of the world, her charity, virginity, and voluntary poverty, are found in the sublimest counsels of Christ and his apostles — suitable to the high expectations of another life, proper instances of a heavenly love, and all followed by the greatest saints of the best and purest ages of the Church.

" He that hath ears to hear, let him hear."

CHAPTER X

The Obligations of
All Men and Women

I HAVE SHOWN that all parts of our life are to be made holy and acceptable unto God. I shall now show that this holiness of common life, this religious use of everything that we have, is a devotion that is the duty of all orders of Christian people.

Everybody acknowledges that all orders of men are to be equally and exactly honest. Now we should find it as absurd to suppose that one man must be exact in piety and another need not as to suppose that one man must be exact in honesty and another need not. Christian humility, sobriety, devotion, and piety are as great and necessary parts of a reasonable life as are justice and honesty.

On the other hand, pride, sensuality, and covetousness are as great disorders of the soul, are as high an abuse of our reason and as contrary to God, as are cheating and dishonesty. Theft and dishonesty seem to vulgar eyes to be greater sins because they are hurtful to civil society and are severely punished by human laws. But if we consider mankind in a higher view, as God's order or society of rational beings, we shall find that every temper that is contrary to reason and order, that opposes God's ends and designs, and that disorders the beauty and glory of the rational world, is equally sinful in man and equally

64

odious to God. This would show us that the sin of sensuality is like the sin of dishonesty and renders us as great objects of the divine displeasure.

Though pride and sensuality do not hurt civil society as do cheating and dishonesty, yet they hurt that society and oppose those ends which are greater and more glorious in the eyes of God than all the societies that relate to this world. If, therefore, you choose to be an idle epicure rather than to be unfaithful; if you choose to live in lust rather than to injure your neighbor, you have no better provision for the favor of God than he who chooses to rob a house rather than to rob a church.

For the abusing of our own nature is as great a disobedience against God as the injuring of our neighbor. He who lacks piety toward God has done as much to damn himself as he who lacks honesty toward men. Every argument, therefore, that proves it necessary for men in all stations of life to be truly honest proves it equally necessary for all men in all stations of life to be truly holy and pious.

Again, another argument may be taken from our obligation to prayer. It is granted that prayer is a duty that belongs to all states and conditions of man. If we inquire into the reason for this we shall find it as good a reason why every state of life is to be made a state of piety and holiness in all its parts.

For the reason we are to pray unto God and to glorify him with hymns and psalms of thanksgiving is this: we are to live wholly unto God and glorify him in all possible ways. It is not because the praises of words or forms of thanksgiving are more particularly parts of piety or more the worship of God than are other things. It is because they are possible ways of expressing our dependence upon God and our obedience and devotion to God.

If this be the reason for verbal praises and thanksgivings to God, then it plainly follows that we are equally obliged to worship and follow God in all other actions that can be called acts of piety and obedience to him. And as actions are of much more significance than words, it must be a much more acceptable worship of God to glorify him in all the actions of our common life than with any little form of words at any particular time. Thus, he who makes it a rule to be content in every part and accident of his life because it comes from God praises God in a much higher manner than he who has some set time for the singing of psalms.

He who dares not say an ill-natured word or do an unreasonable thing because he considers God as everywhere present performs a better devotion than he who dares not miss the church. To live in the world as a stranger and a pilgrim, using all its enjoyments as if we used them not, making all our actions as so many steps toward a better life, is offering a better sacrifice to God than any forms of holy and heavenly prayers.

To be humble in our actions, to avoid every appearance of pride and vanity, to be meek and lowly in our words, actions, dress, behavior, and designs — all in imitation of our blessed Saviour — is worshiping God in a higher manner than do they who have only stated times to fall low on their knees in devotions. He who contents himself with necessities that he may give the remainder to those who need it; who dares not spend any money foolishly because he considers it as a talent from God which must be used according to his will, praises God with something that is more glorious than songs of praise.

He who has appointed times for the use of wise and pious prayers performs a proper instance of devotion. But he who allows himself not times, nor any places, nor any actions, but such as are strictly conformable to wisdom and holiness worships the divine Nature with the most true and substantial devotion. For who does not know that it is better to be pure and holy than to talk about purity and holiness? Who does not know that a man is to be reckoned no more pure, or holy, or just, than he is pure and holy and just in the common course of his life? If this be plain, then it is also plain that it is better to be holy than to have holy prayers. As words are but small things in themselves, as times of prayer are little when compared to the rest of our lives, so that devotion which consists in times and forms of prayer is but a very small thing when compared with that devotion which is to appear in every other part and circumstance of our lives.

Every sober reader will easily perceive that I do not intend to lessen the true and great value of prayers, either public or private, but only to show him that they are certainly but a very slender part of devotion when compared with a devout life. Bended knees while you are clothed with pride; heavenly petitions while you are hoarding up treasures upon the earth; holy devotions while you live in the follies of the world; prayers of meekness and charity while your heart is the seat of pride and resentment; hours of prayer while you give up days and years to idle diversions — are as absurd, unacceptable services to God as forms of thanskgiving from a person who lives in repinings and discontent. Unless the common course of our lives be according to the common spirit of our prayers, our prayers are so far from being a real or sufficient devotion that they become an empty lip labor or, what is worse, a notorious hypocrisy.

This may serve to convince us that all orders of people are to labor and aspire after the same utmost perfection of the Christian life. A soldier or a tradesman is not called to minister at the altar or preach the gospel, but every soldier or tradesman is as much obliged to be devout, holy, and heavenly-minded in all parts of his common life as a clergyman is obliged to be zealous, faithful, and laborious in all parts of his profession. And all this for one plain reason: because all people are to pray for the same holiness, wisdom, and divine tempers and to make themselves as fit as they can for the same heaven.

All men, therefore, as men, have one and the same important business: to act up to the excellency of their rational nature, to make reason and order the law of all their designs and actions. All Christians, as Christians, have one and the same calling: to live according to the excellency of the Christian spirit, to make the sublime precepts of the gospel the rule and measure of all their common life. The one thing needful is the one thing needful to all.

The merchant is no longer to hoard up treasures upon the earth. The scholar is no longer to pride himself in the depths of science. But they must all with one spirit " count all things but loss for the excellency of the knowledge of Christ Jesus."

The fine lady must teach her eyes to weep and be clothed with humility. The polite gentleman must exchange the gay thoughts of wit and fancy for a broken and contrite heart. The man of quality must so far renounce the dignity of his birth as to think himself miserable until he is born again. Servants must consider their service as done unto God. Masters must consider their servants as their brethren in Christ, who are to be treated as their fellow members of the mystical body of Christ.

All must aspire after such a gentility as they might have learned from seeing the blessed Jesus, and show no other spirit but such as they might have received from the holy apostles. They must learn to love God with all their heart, with all their soul, and with all their strength, and their neighbor as themselves. Then they have all the greatness and distinction that they can have here and are fit for an eternal happiness in heaven hereafter. Thus in all orders and conditions, either of men or of women, this is the one common holiness which is to be the common life of all Christians.

The merchant is not to leave devotion to the clergyman, nor the clergyman to leave humility to the laborer. Women of fortune are not to leave it to the poorer of their sex to be discreet, chaste, keepers at home, and to adorn themselves in modest apparel. Nor are poor women to leave it to the rich to attend at the worship and service of God. Great men must be eminent for true poverty of spirit, and people of a low and afflicted state must greatly rejoice in God. The man of strength and power is to forgive and pray for his enemies, and the innocent sufferer chained in prison must, with Paul and Silas, sing praise of God. For God is to be glorified, holiness is to be practiced, and the spirit of religion is to be the common spirit of every Christian in every state and condition of life.

For the Son of God did not come from above to add an external form of worship to the several ways of life that are in the world, and so to leave people to live as they did before. But he came down from heaven altogether divine and heavenly in his own nature to call mankind to a divine and heavenly life; to the highest change of their own nature; to be born again of the Holy Spirit; to walk in the wisdom and light of God; to be like him to the utmost of their power; to renounce all the most plausible ways of the world; and to live in such wisdom, purity, and holiness as might fit them to be glorious in the enjoyment of God to all eternity.

Whatever, therefore, is foolish, ridiculous, vain, earthly, or

sensual in the life of a Christian is something that ought not to
be there. It is a spot and a defilement that must be washed
away with tears of repentance. If anything of this kind runs
through the course of our whole life, we renounce our profession.

For as sure as Jesus Christ was wisdom and holiness, as sure
as he came to make us like himself and to be baptized into his
spirit, so sure is it that none can be said to keep to their Christian profession but they who, to the utmost of their power, live
a wise and holy and heavenly life. This and this alone is Christianity.

Chapter XI

On the Reward of Great Devotion

SOME PEOPLE will perhaps object that all these rules of holy living are too great a restraint upon human life, that by depriving ourselves of so many seemingly innocent pleasures we shall render our lives dull, uneasy, and melancholy. To this it may be answered:

First, that instead of making our lives dull and melancholy they will render them full of content and strong satisfactions. By these rules we only change our childish satisfactions for the solid enjoyments and real happiness of a sound mind.

Secondly, the more we look to God in all our actions, the more we conform to his will; the more we act according to his wisdom and imitate his goodness, by so much the more do we enjoy God and heighten and increase all that is happy and comfortable in human life.

Thirdly, he who is endeavoring to root out of his mind all those passions of pride, envy, and ambition which religion opposes is doing more to make himself happy than he who is contriving means to indulge them. For these passions are the causes of all the disquiets and vexations of human life.

God Almighty has sent us into the world with very few wants. Meat and drink and clothing are the only things necessary in life. And as these are our only present needs the present world is well furnished to supply these needs. This is the state of man — born with few wants into a large world very capable of supplying them. So that one would reasonably suppose that men should pass their lives in contentedness and thankfulness to God. At least, that they should be free from violent disquiets and vexations.

If to all this we add that this short life is only a brief passage to eternal glory where we shall be clothed with the brightness of angels and enter into the joys of God, we might still more reasonably expect that human life should be a state of peace and joy and delight in God.

But, alas! though God and nature and reason make human life thus free from wants and so full of happiness, yet our passions, in rebellion against God, nature, and reason, create a new world of evils. They fill human life with imaginary wants and vain disquiets. The man of pride has a thousand wants which only his pride has created. These render him as full of trouble as if God had created him with a thousand appetites without creating anything that was proper to satisfy them.

If you should see a man who had a large pond of water, yet living in continual thirst for fear of lessening his pond; if you should see him wasting his time and strength in fetching more water to his pond, always carrying a bucket of water in his hand, watching early and late to catch the drops of rain, gaping after every cloud, and running greedily into every mire and mud in hope of water, and always studying how to make every ditch empty itself into his pond; if you should see him grow gray and old in these anxious labors and at last end a careful, thirsty life by falling into his own pond — would you not say that such a one was not only the author of all his own disquiets but was foolish enough to be reckoned among idiots and madmen? But yet foolish and absurd as this character is, he does not represent half the follies and absurd disquiets of the covetous man.

Caelia is always telling you how provoked she is, what intolerable, shocking things happen to her, what monstrous usage she suffers, and what vexations she meets with everywhere. She tells you that her patience is quite worn out and there is no bearing the behavior of people. Every group she attends sends her home provoked — something or other has been said or done that no reasonable, well-bred person ought to bear. Poor people who want her charity are sent away with hasty answers, not because she has no heart to part with her money but because she is too full of some trouble of her own to attend to the complaints of others. Caelia has no business but to receive the income of a plentiful fortune, yet you would be apt to think that she had neither food nor lodging. If you see her look more pale than ordinary, if her lips tremble when she speaks to you, it is because she has just come from a visit where Lupus took no notice at all of her but talked all the time to Lucinda. When cross accidents have so disordered her spirits that she is forced to send for the doctor to make her able to eat, she tells him in great anger at Providence that she never was well since she was born and that she envies beggars whom she sees in health.

This is the disquiet life of Caelia who has nothing to torment her but her own spirit. If you could inspire her with Christian humility you need do no more to make her as happy as any person in the world. This virtue would make her thankful to God for half as much health as she has had and would help her to enjoy more for the time to come.

I have just touched upon these absurd characters for no other end but to convince you that the strictest rules of religion are so far from rendering a life dull, anxious, and uncomfortable that, on the contrary, all the miseries, vexations, and complaints that are in the world are owing to the *lack* of religion. For all the wants that disturb human life; that make us uneasy to ourselves, quarrelsome with others, and unthankful to God; that weary us in vain labors and foolish anxieties; that carry us from project to project, from place to place in a poor pursuit of we know not what — are the wants that neither God nor nature nor reason has subjected us to, but are solely infused into us by pride, envy, and covetousness. So far, therefore, as you reduce your desires to such things as nature and reason require, so far as you regulate all the notions of your heart by the strict rules of religion, so far you remove yourself from that infinity of wants and vexations that torment every heart that is left to itself.

As to those satisfactions and enjoyments which an exalted piety requires us to deny ourselves, this deprives us of no real comfort of life. Let us suppose a person destitute of that knowledge placed somewhere alone in the midst of a variety of things that he did not know how to use — that he has by him bread, wine, water, golden dust, iron chains, gravel, garments, and fire. Let it be supposed that in his thirst he puts golden dust into his eyes; that when his eyes smart he puts wine into his ears; that in his hunger he puts gravel into his mouth; that in pain he loads himself with the iron chains; that feeling cold he puts his feet in the water; that being frightened at the fire he runs away from it; that being weary he makes a seat of bread. Let it be supposed that through his ignorance of the right use of the things that are about him he will vainly torment himself while he lives, and at last die, blinded with dust, choked with gravel, and loaded with irons. Let it be supposed that some good being came to him and showed him the nature and use of all the things that were about him and gave him such strict rules for using them as would certainly, if observed, make him the happier for all that he had and deliver him from the pains of hunger, thirst, and cold. Now could you with any reason affirm that those strict rules of using those things that were about him had rendered that poor man's life dull and uncomfortable?

Now this is in some measure a representation of the strict rules of religion. They only relieve our ignorance, save us from tormenting ourselves, and teach us to use everything about us to our proper advantage. Man is placed in a world full of a variety of things. His ignorance makes him use many of them as absurdly as the man who put dust in his eyes to relieve his thirst or put on chains to remove pain.

Religion, therefore, comes to his relief and gives him strict rules of using everything that is about him in order that he may have always the pleasure of receiving a right benefit from them. It tells him that although this world can do no more for him than satisfy these wants of the body, yet there is a much greater good prepared for man than eating, drinking, and dressing; that it is yet invisible to his eyes, being too glorious for the apprehension of flesh and blood, but reserved for him to enter upon as soon as this short life is over. It tells him that this state of glory will be given to all those who make a right use of the things of this present world, who do not blind themselves with golden dust, or eat gravel, or groan under loads of iron of their own putting on.

Now can anyone say that the strictest rules of such a religion debar us from any of the comforts of life? If religion forbids all instances of revenge, it is because all revenge is of the nature of poison. If religion commands us to love our neighbor as ourselves, it is because all degrees of love are degrees of happiness which strengthen and support the divine life of the soul and are as necessary to its health and happiness as proper food is necessary to the health and happiness of the body. If religion has laws against laying up treasures upon earth and commands us to be content with food and raiment, it is because every other use of the world is abusing it to our own vexation. If religion said, " Sell that thou hast, and give to the poor," it is because there is no other way of making ourselves happier by our riches.

If religion requires us sometimes to fast and to deny our natural appetites, it is to lessen that struggle and war that is in our nature. It is to render our bodies fitter instruments of purity and more obedient to the good motions of divine grace. It is to dry up the springs of our passions that war against the soul, to cool the flame of our blood, and to render the mind more capable of divine meditations.

If religion commands us to live wholly unto God and to do all to his glory, it is because every other way is living wholly against ourselves, and will end in our own shame and confusion of face.

How ignorant, therefore, are they of the nature of religion, of the nature of man, and of the nature of God who think a life of strict piety and devotion to God to be a dull, uncomfortable state — when it is so plain and certain that there is neither comfort nor joy to be found in anything else!

Chapter XII

On the Inventions of Happiness

WE MAY SEE more of the happiness of a life devoted unto God by considering the poor excuses for happiness that people are seeking by other methods. For instance, when a man proposes to be happy in ways of ambition by raising himself to some imaginary heights above other people, he is practicing an invention of happiness which has no foundation in nature. It is as if a man should intend to make himself happy by climbing up a ladder.

If a woman seeks for happiness from fine colors upon her face or from jewels and rich clothes, this is merely an invention of happiness — as contrary to nature and reason as if she should propose to make herself happy by painting a post and putting the same finery upon it. It is in this respect that I call these joys mere inventions of happiness because neither God nor nature nor reason has appointed them as such. Whatever appears joyful or great or happy in them is entirely created or invented by the blindness and vanity of our own minds. And it is on these inventions of happiness that I desire you to cast your eye, that you may learn how great a good religion is.

Look at Flatus and learn how miserable are they who are left to the folly of their own passions. Flatus is rich and in health, yet is always uneasy and is always searching after happiness.

Every time you visit him you find some new project in his head. At first fine clothes were his delight. His inquiry was only after the best tailors and he had no thoughts of excelling in anything but dress. But when this happiness did not answer his expectations he left off his brocades, put on a plain coat, railed at fops and beaux, and gave himself up to gaming with great eagerness. This new pleasure satisfied him for some time. He envied no other way of life. But being by the fate of play drawn into a duel where he narrowly escaped his death, he left off the dice and sought for happiness among the diversions of the town. For more than a year you heard him talk of nothing but ladies, drawing rooms, plays, balls, and assemblies. But, growing sick of these, he had recourse to hard drinking. Here he had many a merry night and met with stronger joys than any he had felt before. But, unluckily falling into a fever, he grew angry at all strong liquors and took his leave of the happiness of being drunk.

The next attempt after happiness carried him into the field. For two or three years nothing was so happy as hunting. He entered upon it with all his soul, and leaped more hedges and ditches than had ever been known in so short a time. You never saw him but in a green coat. He was the envy of all who blew the horn, and he always spoke to his dogs in great propriety of language.

No sooner had Flatus outdone all the world in the breed and education of his dogs, built new kennels and new stables, and bought a new hunting seat, but he immediately got sight of another happiness. He hated the senseless noise and hurry of hunting, gave away the dogs, and was deep in the pleasures of building. Now he invents new kinds of dovecotes and has such contrivances in his barns and stables as were never seen before.

He wonders at the dullness of the old builders, is wholly bent upon the improvement of architecture, and will hardly hang a door in the ordinary way. He tells his friends that he never was so delighted in anything in his life — that he has more happiness among his bricks and mortar than he ever had at court.

The next year he leaves his house unfinished, complains to everybody of masons and carpenters, and devotes himself wholly to the happiness of riding about. After this, you can never see him but on horseback. A variety of new saddles and bridles, and a great change of horses, added much to the pleasure of his new way of life. But, having after some time tired both himself and his horses, the happiest thing he could think of next was to go abroad and visit foreign countries. There indeed happiness exceeded his imagination, and he was only uneasy that he had not begun so fine a life sooner. The next month he returned home, however, unable to bear any longer the impertinence of foreigners.

After this, he was a great student for one whole year. He was up early and late at his Italian grammar that he might have the happiness of understanding the opera whenever he should hear one.

Flatus is now doing what he never did in his life before: he is reasoning and reflecting with himself. He loses several days in considering which of his cast-off ways of life he shall try again. But here a new project takes his fancy. He is now living upon herbs and running about the country to get himself into as good wind as any running footman in the kingdom.

I have been thus circumstantial in so many foolish particulars of this kind of life because I hope that every particular folly that you here see will naturally turn itself into an argument for the wisdom and happiness of a religious life.

But you will perhaps say that the ridiculous, restless life of Flatus is not the common state of those who resign themselves to live by their own humors and neglect the strict rules of religion — that therefore it is not so great an argument for the happiness of a religious life as I would make it.

I answer that I am afraid that Flatus is one of the most general characters in life, and that few people can read of him without seeing something in him that belongs to themselves. For where shall we find that wise and happy man who has not been eagerly pursuing different appearances of happiness — sometimes thinking it was here and sometimes there?

But, secondly, let it be granted that most people are not of such restless and fickle tempers as Flatus. The difference, then, is only this: Flatus is continually changing and trying something new, but others are content with some one state. They do not leave gaming and then fall to hunting. They have so much steadiness in their tempers that some seek after no other happiness than that of heaping up riches. Others grow old in the sports of the field. Others are content to drink themselves to death, without the least inquiry after any other happiness.

Now, is there anything more happy or reasonable in such a life as this than in the life of Flatus? Shall religion be looked upon as a burden, as a dull and melancholy state, for calling men from such " happiness " as this to live according to the laws of God, to labor after the perfection of their nature, and to prepare themselves for an endless state of joy and glory in the presence of God?

Look at the poor condition of Succus, whose greatest happiness is a good night's rest in bed and a good meal when he is up. When he talks of happiness it is always in such expressions as show you that he has only his bed and his dinner in his thoughts.

His regard to his meals and repose makes Succus order all the rest of his time with relation to them. He will undertake no business that may break in upon his hours of eating and rest. If he reads, it shall be for half an hour and he will read something that may make him laugh — as rendering the body fitter for its food and rest. If he has, at any time, a mind to indulge a serious thought he always has recourse to a useful treatise upon ancient cookery. Succus is an enemy to all political matters, having made an observation that there is as good eating among the Whigs as among the Tories.

All the hours that are not devoted to either repose or nourishment are looked upon by Succus as waste or spare time. For this reason, he lodges near a coffeehouse and a tavern, that when he rises in the morning he may be near the news and when he parts at night he may not have far to go to bed.

If you were to live with Succus for a year this is all that you would see in his life.

Who can help blessing God for the means of grace and for the hope of glory when he sees what variety of folly they sink into who live without it? Who would not heartily be " steadfast, unmovable, always abounding in the work of the Lord " when he sees what dull sensuality, what poor views, what gross enjoyments, they are left to who seek for happiness in other ways?

Consider now how unreasonable it is to pretend that a life of strict piety must be a dull state. Must it be tedious and tiresome to live in the continual practice of love, to act wisely and virtuously, to do good to the utmost of your power, to imitate the divine perfections, and to prepare yourself for the enjoyment of God? Must it be dull and tiresome to be delivered from blindness and vanity, from false hopes and vain fears? Must it be tedious and dull to feel the comforts of conscience in all your actions, to know that God is your Friend, to know that neither life nor death can do you any harm? Must such a state as this be dull and tedious and tiresome for lack of such "happiness" as Flatus or Succus enjoys?

Now if this cannot be said, the devout man has nothing to envy in any other state of life. For without religion all the art and contrivance in the world cannot make more of human life, or carry its happiness to any greater height, than Flatus and Succus have done.

If you were to see a man dully endeavoring all his life to satisfy his thirst by holding up one and the same empty cup to his mouth, you would certainly think him ignorant. But if you should see others of finer understanding ridiculing the dull satisfaction of one cup and thinking of satisfying their own thirst by a variety of gilt and golden empty cups, would you think that these were any wiser, or happier, or better employed? The dull and heavy soul may be content with one empty appearance of happiness, and be continually trying to hold one and the same empty cup to his mouth all his life. But then let the wit, the great scholar, the fine genius, the great statesman, the polite gentleman lay all their heads together, and they can only show you more and various empty appearances of happiness. Give them all the world into their hands, let them cut and carve as they please, and they can only make a greater variety of empty cups. And if all that is in the world is only so many empty cups, what does it signify which you take, or how many you take, or how many you have?

This is the wisdom that cries and puts forth her voice in the streets, that stands at all our doors, that appeals to all our senses, teaching us in everything and everywhere by all that we see and all that we hear, by births and burials, by sickness and health, by life and death, by pains and poverty, by misery and vanity, and by all the changes and chances of life, that there is nothing else for man to look for, no other end for him to drive toward, than a happiness that is to be found only in the hopes and expectations of religion.

Chapter XIII

The Emptiness of a Life
Not Governed by Devotion

IT IS a very remarkable saying of our Lord: "Blessed are your eyes, for they see: and your ears, for they hear." They teach us two things: first, that the dullness and heaviness of men's minds with regard to spiritual matters is so great that it may justly be compared to the lack of eyes and ears. Secondly, that God has so filled everything and every place with motives and arguments for a godly life that they who are so blessed as to use their eyes and their ears must needs be affected with them.

Now though this was, in a more especial manner, the case of those whose senses were witnesses of the life, miracles, and doctrines of our blessed Lord, yet it is truly the case of all Christians at this time. For the reasons of religion are so written and engraved upon everything, and present themselves so strongly and so constantly to all our senses in everything that we meet, that they can be disregarded only by eyes that see not and ears that hear not.

What greater motive to a religious life than the vanity, the poorness, of all worldly enjoyments? What greater call to look toward God than the pains, the sickness, the crosses and vexations, of this life? What miracles could more strongly appeal to our senses or what message from heaven speak louder to us than the daily dying and departure of our fellow creatures? So that the one thing needful, or the great end of life, is not left to be discovered by fine reasoning and deep reflections. It is pressed upon us in the plainest manner by the experience of all our senses, by everything that we meet with in life.

Octavius is a learned, ingenious man, well versed in most parts of literature, and no stranger to any kingdom of Europe. The other day, being just recovered from a lingering fever, he took upon him to talk thus to his friends:

" My glass," says he, " is almost run out! Your eyes see how many marks of age and death I bear about me, but I plainly feel myself sinking away faster than any standers-by imagine. I fully believe that one year more will conclude my reckoning."

The attention of his friends was much raised by such a declaration, expecting to hear something truly excellent from so learned a man who had but a year longer to live. Then Octavius proceeded in this manner: "For these reasons, my friends, I have left off all taverns — the wine of those places is not good enough for me in this decay of nature. I must now be nice in what I drink. Therefore, I am resolved to furnish my own cellar with a little of the very best, though it cost me ever so much.

" I must also tell you, my friends, that age forces a man to be wise in many other respects and makes us change many of our opinions and practices. You know how much I have liked a large acquaintance. I now condemn it as an error. Three or four cheerful, diverting companions are all that I now desire. I find that in my present infirmities if I am left alone, or to grave company, I am not so easy to myself."

A few days after Octavius had made this declaration to his friends, he relapsed into his former illness, was committed to a nurse, who closed his eyes before his fresh parcel of wine came in.

Young Eugenius, who was present at this discourse, went home a new man with full resolutions of devoting himself wholly unto God. "I never," says Eugenius, "was so deeply affected with the wisdom and importance of religion as when I saw how poorly and meanly the learned Octavius was to leave the world. How often had I envied his great learning, his skill in languages, his knowledge of antiquity, his address and fine manner of expressing himself upon all subjects! But when I saw how poorly it all ended, how foolishly the master of all these accomplishments was then forced to talk for want of being acquainted with the joys and expectations of piety, I was thoroughly convinced that there was nothing to be envied or desired but a life of true piety — nor anything so poor and comfortless as a death without it."

Now as the young Eugenius was thus edified and instructed in the present case, so you — if you are so happy as to have anything of his thoughtful temper — will find that arguments for the wisdom and happiness of a strict piety offer themselves in all places and appeal to all your senses in the plainest manner. You will find that all the world preaches to an attentive mind. And if you have but ears to hear, almost anything you meet teaches you some lesson of wisdom.

Cognatus is a sober, regular clergyman, of good repute in the world and well esteemed in his parish. All his parishioners say he is an honest man and very notable at making a bargain. The farmers listen to him with great attention when he talks of the best time to sell corn. He has been for twenty years a diligent observer of markets and has raised a considerable fortune by good management. Cognatus is very orthodox and full of esteem for our English liturgy. If he has not prayers on Wednesdays and Fridays it is because his predecessor had not accustomed the parish to any such custom.

Since he cannot serve both his livings himself, he makes it a matter of conscience to keep a sober curate upon one of them, whom he hires to take care of all the souls in the parish at as cheap a rate as a sober man can be procured.

Cognatus has been very prosperous all his time, but still he has had the uneasiness and vexations that they have who are deep in worldly business. Taxes, losses, bad mortgages, bad tenants, and the hardness of the times are frequent subjects of his conversation. A good or bad season has a great effect upon his spirits.

Cognatus has no other end in growing rich but that he may leave a considerable fortune to a niece, whom he has educated in expensive finery by what he has saved out of the tithes of two livings.

The neighbors look upon Cognatus as a happy clergyman because they see him (as they call it) in good circumstances. Some of them intend to dedicate their own sons to the Church because they see how well it has succeeded with Cognatus, whose father was but an ordinary man.

If instead of rejoicing in the happiness of a second living he had thought it as unbecoming the office of a clergyman to traffic for gain in holy things as to open a shop; if he had thought it better to recommend some honest labor to his niece than to support her in idleness by the labors of a curate; if he had thought it better that she should lack fine clothes and a rich husband than that cures of souls should be farmed about— if this had been the spirit of Cognatus, could it with any reason be said that these rules of religion, this strictness of piety, had robbed Cognatus of any real happiness? Could it be said that a life thus governed by the spirit of the gospel must be dull and melancholy when compared to that of raising a fortune for a niece?

Now as this cannot be said in the present case, so in every other kind of life you will find that however easy and prosperous it may seem, yet you cannot add piety to any part of it without adding so much of a better joy and happiness to it.

Look now at the condition of life that draws the envy of all eyes.

Negotius is a temperate, honest man. He served his time under a master of great trade, but has, by his own management, made it a more considerable business than ever it was before. For thirty years he has written fifty or sixty letters in a week, and is busy in corresponding with all parts of Europe. The general good of trade seems to Negotius to be the general good of life. Whomever he admires, whatever he commends or condemns either in Church or State, is admired, commended, or condemned with some regard to trade. As money is continually pouring in upon him, he often lets it go in various kinds of expense and generosity, and sometimes in ways of charity.

Negotius is always ready to join in any public contribution. If a purse is being made at any place where he happens to be, whether it be to buy a plate for a horse race or to redeem a prisoner out of gaol, you are always sure of having something from him.

If Negotius were asked what it is that he drives at in life, he would be as much at a loss for an answer as if he were asked what any other person is thinking of. For though he always seems to himself to know what he is doing and has many things in his head, yet he cannot tell you of any one general end in life.

The generality of people, when they think of happiness, think of Negotius, in whose life every instance of happiness is supposed to meet: sober, prudent, rich, prosperous, generous, and charitable.

Let us now, therefore, look at this condition in another but truer light.

Let it be supposed that this same Negotius were a laborious man deep in a variety of affairs; that he neither drank nor debauched, but was sober and regular in his business. Let it be supposed that he grew old in this course of trading, and that the end and design of all his labor and application to business were only this: that he might die possessed of more than a hundred thousand pairs of boots and spurs and as many greatcoats. Let it be supposed that the sober part of the world say of him, when he is dead, that he was a great and happy man, a thorough master of business, and had acquired a hundred thousand pairs of boots and spurs when he died.

Now if this were really the case, I believe it would be readily granted that a life of such business was as poor and ridiculous as any that can be invented. But it would puzzle anyone to show that a man has spent all his time and thoughts in business and hurry that he might die worth a hundred thousand pounds is any whit wiser than he who has taken the same pains to have as many pairs of boots and spurs when he leaves the world.

For if the only end of life be to die as free from sin and as exalted in virtue as we can; if naked as we came, so naked are we to return and to stand a trial before Christ and his holy angels, for everlasting happiness or misery — what can it possibly signify what a man had or had not in this world? What can it signify what you call those things which a man has left behind him? I say, call them; for the things signify no more to him than the names.

Let it therefore be supposed that instead of continual hurry of business he was frequent in his retirements and a strict observer of all the hours of prayer; that instead of restless desires after more riches his soul has been full of the love of God, constantly watching against worldly tempers and always aspiring after divine grace; that instead of worldly cares and contrivances he was busy in fortifying his soul against all approaches of sin; that instead of costly show and expensive generosity of a splendid life he loved and exercised all instances of humility and lowliness; that instead of great treats and full tables his house only furnished a sober refreshment to those who lacked it. Let it be supposed that his contentment kept him free from all kinds of envy; that his piety made him thankful to God in all crosses and disappointments; that his charity kept him from being rich by a continual distribution to all objects of compassion. Had this been the Christian spirit of Negotius, can anyone say that he had lost the true joy and happiness of life by thus conforming to the spirit and living up to the hopes of the gospel? Can it be said that a life made exemplary by such virtues as these, which both delight and exalt the soul here and prepare it for the presence of God hereafter, must be poor and dull if compared to that of heaping up riches, which can neither stay with us nor we with them?

It would be endless to multiply examples of this kind to show how little is lost and how much is gained by introducing a strict and exact piety into every condition of human life. I shall now, therefore, leave it to your own meditation, hoping that you are enough directed to convince yourself that a true and exalted piety is so far from rendering any life dull and tiresome that it is the only joy and happiness of every condition in the world.

Chapter XIV

On the Times and Hours
of Prayer

HAVING SHOWN the necessity of a devout spirit in every part of our common life, I come now to consider that part of devotion which relates to times and hours of prayer.

Prayer is the nearest approach to God and the highest enjoyment of him that we are capable of in this life. It is as much your duty to rise to pray as to pray when you are risen. And if you are late at your prayers you offer to God the prayers of an idle, slothful worshiper who rises to prayers as idle servants rise to their labor.

What conquest has he got over himself? What right hand has he cut off, what trials is he prepared for, what sacrifice is he ready to offer unto God, who cannot be so cruel to himself as to rise to prayer at such time as the drudging part of the world are content to rise to their labor?

This much, I believe, is certain: the generality of Christians ought to use forms of prayer at all the regular times of prayer. It seems right for everyone to begin with a form of prayer. If, in the midst of his devotions, he finds his heart ready to break forth into new and higher strains of devotion, he should leave his form for a while and follow those fervors of his heart till it again wants the assistance of his usual petitions. This seems to be the true liberty of private devotion. It should be under the direction of some form, but not so tied down to it but that it may be free to take such new expressions as its present fervors happen to furnish it with — which sometimes are more affecting and carry the soul more powerfully to God than any expressions that were ever used before.

Sometimes the light of God's countenance shines so bright upon us, we see so far into the invisible world, we are so affected with the wonders of the love and goodness of God, that our hearts worship and adore in a language higher than that of words, and we feel transports of devotion which only can be felt.

The first thing that you are to do when you are upon your knees is to shut your eyes. Then with a short silence let your soul place itself in the presence of God. That is, you are to use this or some other better method to separate yourself from all common thoughts, and make your heart as sensible as you can of the divine presence.

To proceed: if you were to accustom yourself to pray always in the same place; if you were to reserve that place for devotion and not allow yourself to do anything common in it; if you were never to be there but in times of devotion; if any little room or, if that cannot be, if any particular part of a room was thus used, this kind of consecration of it as a place holy unto God would have such an effect upon your mind as would very much assist your devotion. A place thus sacred in your room would in some measure resemble a chapel or house of God. This would dispose you to be always in the spirit of religion when you were there, and fill you with wise and holy thoughts when you were by yourself. Your own apartment would raise in your mind such sentiments as you have when you stand near an altar. You would be afraid of thinking or doing anything that was foolish near that place, which is the place of prayer and holy intercourse with God.

As the morning is to you the beginning of a new life, as God has then given you a new enjoyment of yourself and a fresh entrance into the world, it is highly proper that your first devotions should be a praise and thanksgiving to God, as for a new creation. You should offer and devote body and soul, all that you are and all that you have, to his service and glory. Receive, therefore, every day as a resurrection from death, as a new enjoyment of life. Meet every rising sun with such sentiments of God's goodness as if you had seen it, and all things, new created upon your account. And under the sense of so great a blessing, let your joyful heart praise and magnify so good and glorious a Creator.

Let, therefore, praise and thanksgiving and oblation of yourself unto God be always the fixed and certain subject of your first prayers in the morning. And then take the liberty of adding such other devotions as the accidental difference of your state or of your heart shall make most needful and expedient for you. For one of the greatest benefits of private devotion consists in rightly adapting our prayers to those two conditions: the difference of our state and the difference of our hearts.

By the difference of our state is meant the difference of our external condition — as of sickness, health, pains, losses, disappointments, troubles, particular mercies or judgments from God, and all sorts of kindnesses, injuries, or reproaches from other people. Now as these are great parts of our state of life, so our devotion will be made doubly beneficial to us when it watches to receive and sanctify all these changes of our state and turns them all into so many occasions of a more particular application to God of such thanksgiving, such resignation, such petitions, as our present state more especially requires. And he who makes every change in his state a reason of presenting unto God some particular petitions suitable to that change will soon find that he has taken an excellent means not only of praying with fervor, but of living as he prays.

The next condition to which we are always to adapt some part of our prayers is the different state of the tempers of our hearts — as of love, joy, peace, tranquillity, dullness and dryness of spirit, anxiety, discontent, motions of envy and ambition, dark and disconsolate thoughts, resentments, fretfulness, and peevish tempers. If we are in the delightful calm of sweet and easy passions, of love and joy in God, we should then offer the grateful tribute of thanksgiving to God for the possession of so much happiness, thankfully owning and acknowledging him as the bountiful Giver of it all.

If, on the other hand, we feel ourselves laden with heavy passions, with dullness of spirit, anxiety, and uneasiness, we must then look up to God in acts of humility, confessing our unworthiness, opening our troubles to him, beseeching him in his good time to lessen the weight of our infirmities, and to deliver us from such passions as oppose the purity and perfection of our souls.

Mundanus is a man of clear apprehension. He is well advanced in age and has made a great figure in business. Every part of trade and business that has fallen in his way has had some improvement from him, and he is always contriving to carry every method of doing anything well to its greatest height. Mundanus aims at the greatest perfection in everything. The soundness and strength and his mind and his just way of thinking upon things make him intent upon removing all imperfections. He can tell you all the defects and errors in all the common methods — whether of trade, building, or improving land or manufactures. The clearness and strength of his understanding, which he is constantly improving by often digesting his thoughts in writing and trying everything every way, has rendered him a great master of most concerns in human life. Thus has Mundanus gone on increasing his knowledge and judgment as fast as his years came upon him.

The only thing that has not fallen under his improvement is his devotion. This is in just the same poor state that it was when he was six years of age, and the old man prays now in that little form of words which his mother used to hear him repeat night and morning. This Mundanus, who hardly ever saw the poorest utensil or ever took the meanest trifle into his hand without considering how it might be made or used to better advantage, has gone all his life long praying in the same manner as when he was a child — without ever considering how much better or oftener he might pray; without considering how improvable the spirit of devotion is, how many helps a wise and reasonable man may call to his assistance, and how necessary it is that our prayers should be enlarged, varied, and suited to the particular state and condition of our lives. If Mundanus sees a book of devotion he passes it by as he does a spelling book, because he remembers that he learned to pray, so many years ago, under his mother, when he learned to spell.

How poor and pitiable is the conduct of this man of sense, who has so much judgment and understanding in everything but that which is the whole wisdom of man!

Classicus is a man of learning and well versed in all the best authors of antiquity. He has read them so much that he has entered into their spirit and can very ingeniously imitate the manner of any of them. All their thoughts are his thoughts.

Classicus tells a young scholar that he must not think he has done enough when he has only learned languages. He must be daily conversant with the best authors, read them again and again, catch their spirit by living with them, and that there is no other way of becoming like them, or of making himself a man of taste and judgment.

How wise might Classicus have been and how much good might he have done in the world, if he had but thought as justly of devotion as he does of learning! He never, indeed, says anything shocking or offensive about devotion, because he never thinks or talks about it. It suffers nothing from him but neglect and disregard. The two Testaments would not have had so much as a place among his books but that they are both to be had in Greek. Classicus thinks that he sufficiently shows his regard for the Holy Scriptures when he tells you that he has no other books of piety besides them.

Now if you were to ask Mundanus and Classicus, or any man of business or learning, whether piety is not the highest perfection of man or devotion the greatest attainment in the world, they must both be forced to answer in the affirmative or else give up the truth of the gospel. For to set any accomplishment against devotion is the same absurdity in a Christian as it would be in a philosopher to prefer a meal's meat to the greatest improvement in knowledge. For as philosophy professes purely the search and inquiry after knowledge, so Christianity supposes, intends, desires, and aims at nothing else but the raising of fallen man to a divine life, to such habits of holiness, such degrees of devotion as may fit him to enter among the holy inhabitants of the Kingdom of Heaven.

To conclude this chapter: Devotion is nothing else but right apprehensions and right affections toward God. All practices, therefore, that heighten and improve our true apprehensions of God, all ways of life that tend to nourish, raise, and fix our affections upon him are to be reckoned so many helps and means to fill us with devotion.

As prayer is the proper fuel of this holy flame, so we must use all our care and contrivance to give prayer its full power — as by alms, self-denial, frequent retirements, holy readings, composing forms for ourselves or using the best we can get, adding length of time, and observing hours of prayer: changing, improving, and suiting our devotions to the condition of our lives and the state of our hearts.

Those who have most leisure seem more especially called to a more eminent observance of these holy rules of a devout life. And they who, by the necessity of their state and not through their own choice, have but little time to employ thus, must make the best use of that little they have. For this is the certain way of making devotion produce a devout life.

Chapter XV

*The Singing of Psalms
in Our Private Devotions*

YOU HAVE SEEN in the foregoing chapter what means and methods you are to use to raise and improve your devotions. There is one thing still remaining which cannot be neglected without great injury to your devotions: to begin all your prayers with a psalm.

There is nothing that so clears a way for your prayers, nothing that so disperses dullness of heart, nothing that so purifies the soul from poor and little passions, nothing that so opens heaven or carries your heart so near it as these songs of praise. They create a sense of delight in God; they awaken holy desires; they teach how to ask; and they prevail with God to give. They kindle a holy flame; they turn your heart into an altar; they turn your prayers into incense and carry them as sweet-smelling savor to the throne of grace.

You will perhaps say that singing is a particular talent that belongs only to particular people, and that you have neither voice nor ear to make any music. If you had said that singing is a general talent and that people differ in that as they do in all other things, you had said something much truer. How vastly do people differ in the talent of thinking, which is not only common to all men but seems to be the very essence of human nature! How readily do some people reason upon every-

thing and how hardly do others reason upon anything! Yet
no one desires to be excused from thought or reason because
he does not have these talents as some people have them. But
it is fully as just for a person to think himself excused from
thinking upon God and from reasoning about his duty to him
as for a person to think himself excused from singing the
praises of God because he does not have a fine ear or a musical
voice. As it is speaking and not *graceful* speaking that is a required part of prayer; as it is bowing and not *genteel* bowing
that is a proper sort of adoration; so it is singing and not *artful*
or *fine* singing that is a required way of praising God.

This objection might be of some weight if you were desired
to sing to entertain other people, but it is not to be admitted in
the present case where you are required only to sing the praises
of God as a part of your private devotion. Our blessed Saviour
and his apostles sang a hymn, but it may be reasonably supposed that they rejoiced in God rather than made fine music.

Do but live so that your heart may truly rejoice in God and
then you will find that this state of your heart will lack neither
voice nor ear to find a tune for a psalm. Everyone at some time
or other finds himself able to sing in some degree — there are
some times and occasions of joy that make all people ready to
express their sense of it in some sort of harmony. The joy that
they feel forces them to let their voice have a part in it. He,
therefore, who says that he lacks a voice or an ear to sing a
psalm mistakes the case. He lacks that spirit which really rejoices in God. The dullness is in his heart and not in his ear.
When his heart feels a true joy in God, when it has a full relish
of what is expressed in the psalms, he will find it very pleasant
to make the motions of his voice express the motions of his
heart.

Imagine to yourself that you had been with Moses when he was led through the Red Sea; that you had seen the waters divide themselves and stand on a heap on both sides; that you had seen them held up till you had passed through. Do you think that you would then have lacked a voice or an ear to sing with Moses, " The Lord is my strength and song, and he is become my salvation "? I know your own heart tells you that all people must have been singers upon such an occasion. Let this, therefore, teach you that it is the heart that tunes a voice to sing the praises of God, and that if you cannot sing the same words now with joy it is because you are not so affected by the salvation of the world by Jesus Christ as the Jews were, or you yourself would have been, by their deliverance at the Red Sea.

Thus if you can find a man whose heart is full of God, his voice will rejoice in those songs of praise which glorify God. If you, therefore, would delightfully perform this part of devotion, it is not so necessary to learn a tune or practice upon notes as to prepare your heart. If you can once say with David, " My heart is fixed, O God, my heart is fixed," it will be very easy and natural to add, as he did, " I will sing and give praise! "

If, therefore, you would know the reason and necessity of singing psalms you must consider the reason and necessity of praising and rejoicing in God. Singing of psalms is as much the true exercise and support of the spirit of thanksgiving as prayer is the true exercise and support of the spirit of devotion. You may as well think that you can be as devout as you ought without the use of prayer as that you can rejoice in God as you ought without the practice of singing psalms — because this singing is as much the natural language of praise and thanksgiving as prayer is the natural language of devotion.

I have been long upon this subject because of its great importance to true religion. There is no state of mind so holy, so excellent, and so truly perfect as that of thankfulness to God. Consequently, nothing is of more importance in religion than that which exercises and improves this habit of mind. The greatest saint in the world is he who is always thankful to God, who wills everything that God wills, who receives everything as an instance of God's goodness, and who has a heart always ready to praise God for it. All prayer and devotion, fasting and repentance, meditation and retirement, all sacraments and ordinances are but so many means to render the soul thus divine. This is the perfection of all virtues. You need not wonder, therefore, that I lay so much stress upon singing a psalm at all your devotions since you see it is to form your spirit to such joy and thankfulness to God as is the highest perfection of a divine and holy life.

If anyone would tell you the shortest, surest way to all happiness and all perfection, he must tell you to make a rule to yourself to thank and praise God for everything that happens to you. It is certain that whatever seeming calamity happens to you, if you thank and praise God for it you turn it into a blessing. If you could work miracles, therefore, you could not do more for yourself than by this thankful spirit. It heals and turns all that it touches into happiness.

For this reason I exhort you to this method in your devotion that every day may be made a day of thanksgiving, and that the spirit of murmur and discontent may be unable to enter into the heart that is so often employed in singing the praises of God. For who would not be often doing in the day that which St. Paul and Silas would not neglect in the middle of the night? And if, when you are thus singing, it would come into your head how the prison shook and the doors opened when St. Paul sang, it would do your devotion no harm.

Lastly, seeing that our imaginations have great power over our hearts and can mightily affect us with their representations, it would be of great use to you if, at the beginning of your devotions, you were to imagine to yourself some such representation as might heat and warm your heart into a temper suitable to those prayers that you are then about to offer unto God. Thus, before you begin your psalm of praise and rejoicing in God, make this use of your imagination:

Be still. Imagine to yourself that you see the heavens open and the glorious choirs of cherubims and seraphims about the throne of God. Imagine that you hear the music of those angelic voices that cease not day and night to sing the glories of Him who is and was and is to come.

Help your imagination with such passages of Scripture as these: " After this I beheld, and, lo, a great multitude, which no man could number, of all nations, and kindreds, and people, and tongues, stood before the throne, and before the Lamb, clothed with white robes, and palms in their hands; And cried with a loud voice, saying, Salvation to our God which sitteth upon the throne, and unto the Lamb. And all the angels stood round about the throne, and about the elders and the four beasts, and fell before the throne on their faces, and worshipped God. Saying, Amen: Blessing, and glory, and wisdom, and thanksgiving, and honor, and power, and might, be unto our God for ever and ever, Amen."

Think upon this till your imagination has carried you above the clouds; till it has placed you among those heavenly beings and made you long to bear a part in their eternal music.

If you will but accustom yourself to this method you will

soon find it to be an excellent means of raising the spirit of devotion within you. Always, therefore, begin your psalm or song of praise with these imaginations. At every verse of it imagine yourself among those heavenly companions, that your voice is added to theirs, that angels join with you and you with them, that you with a poor and low voice are singing on earth what they are singing in heaven.

Again, sometimes imagine that you had been one of those who joined with our blessed Saviour when he sang a hymn. Strive to imagine with what majesty he looked. Fancy that you had stood close by him surrounded with his glory. Think how your heart would have been inflamed, what ecstasies of joy you would have felt when singing with the Son of God. Think again and again with what joy and devotion you would then have sung had this been your happy state, and what a punishment you should have thought it to be silent. Let this teach you how to be affected by psalms and hymns of thanksgiving.

Again, sometimes imagine to yourself that you see David with his hands upon his harp and his eyes fixed upon heaven, calling in transport upon all the creation — sun and moon, light and darkness, day and night, men and angels — to join with his rapturous soul in praising the Lord of heaven. Dwell upon this imagination till you think you are singing with this divine musician and let such a companion teach you to exalt your heart unto God.

These following psalms are such as wonderfully set forth the glory of God: 34, 96, 103, 111, 145, 146, and 147. You may keep to any one of them at any particular hour, or you may take the finest parts of any psalm and so adding them together may make them more fit for your own devotion.

Chapter XVI

The Virtue and Discipline
of Humility

I COME NOW to the hour of prayer which in Scripture is called
the third hour of the day, but according to our way it is
called the ninth hour of the morning. The devout Christian
must at this time look upon himself as called upon by God to
renew his acts of prayer and address himself again to the throne
of grace. In the last chapter I have laid before you the excellency of praise and thanksgiving and recommend that as
the subject of your first devotions in the morning. And now
because a humble state of soul is the very state of religion, because humility is the life and soul of piety, the foundation and
support of every virtue and good work, and the best guard and
security of all holy affections, I shall recommend humility to
you as highly proper to be made the constant subject of your
devotions at this third hour of the day.

We may as well think to see without eyes or live without
breath as to live in the spirit of religion without the spirit of
humility. Although humility is thus the soul and essence of all
religious duties, it is generally speaking the least understood, the
least regarded, the least intended, the least desired, and the
least sought after, of all virtues.

No people have more occasion to be afraid of the approaches

of pride than those who have made some advances in a pious life. For pride can grow upon our virtues as well as upon our vices, and steals upon us on all occasions. Every good thought that we have, every good action that we do, lays us open to pride and exposes us to the assaults of vanity and self-satisfaction. It is for this reason that I so earnestly advise every devout person to begin every day in this exercise of humility, that he may go on in safety under the protection of this good guide and not fall a sacrifice to his own progress in those virtues which are to save mankind from destruction.

Humility does not consist in having a worse opinion of ourselves than we deserve, nor in abasing ourselves lower than we really are. Rather, as all virtue is founded in truth, so humility is founded in a true and just sense of our weakness, misery, and sin. He who rightly feels and lives in this sense of his condition lives in humility.

The weakness of our state appears from our inability to do anything of ourselves. In our natural state we are entirely without any power and can act only by a power that is every moment lent us from God. Since we neither are nor can be anything of ourselves, to be proud of anything that we are or of anything that we do and to ascribe glory to ourselves for these things has the guilt both of stealing and of lying. It has the guilt of stealing as it gives to ourselves those things which only belong to God. It has the guilt of lying as it is the denying of the truth of our state and pretending to be something that we are not.

Secondly, let a man but consider that if the world knew all of him that he knows of himself — if they saw what vanity and passions govern him inside and what secret tempers sully and corrupt his best actions — he would have no more pretense to be honored and admired for his goodness and wisdom than a rotten and distempered body to be loved and admired for its beauty and comeliness. This is so true and so known to the hearts of almost all people that nothing would appear more dreadful to them than to have their hearts thus fully discovered to the eyes of all beholders. Shall pride be entertained in a heart thus conscious of its own miserable behavior? Shall a creature in such a condition that he could not support himself under the shame of being known to the world in his real state — shall such a creature in the sight of God dare to be vain and proud of himself?

Thirdly, if we add to this the shame and guilt of sin, we shall find a still greater reason for humility. No creature that had lived in innocence would have thereby developed any pretense for self-honor and esteem, because as a creature all that it is, or has, or does, is from God and therefore the honor of all that belongs to it is due only to God. But if a creature that is a sinner and under the displeasure of the great Governor of all the world, and deserving nothing from him but pains and punishments for the shameful abuse of his powers, if such a creature pretends to self-glory for anything that he is or does, he can only be said to glory in his shame.

The monstrous and shameful nature of sin is sufficiently apparent from that great atonement which is necessary to cleanse us from the guilt of it. Nothing less has been required than the sufferings and death of the Son of God. Had he not taken our nature upon him, our nature would have been forever separated from God and incapable of ever appearing before him. And is there any room for pride, for self-glory, while we are partakers of such a nature as this? Shall we presume to take delight in our worth, we who are not worthy so much as to ask pardon for our sins without the mediation and intercession of the Son of God?

Thus deep is the foundation of humility laid in these deplorable circumstances of our condition which show that it is as great an offense against truth to lay claim to any degrees of glory as to pretend to the honor of creating ourselves. If a man will boast of anything as his own, he must boast of his misery and sin, for there is nothing else but this that is his own property.

These are the reflections that you are to meditate upon that you may be disposed to walk before God and man in such a spirit of humility as is becoming to the weak, miserable, sinful state of all who are descended from Adam. When you have by such general reflections as these convinced your mind of the reasonableness of humility, you must not content yourself as if you were therefore humble. But you must immediately enter yourself into the practice of this virtue like a young beginner who has all of it to learn and who can learn but little at a time and with great difficulty. You must consider that you have not only this virtue to learn, but that you must be content to proceed as a learner in it all your time, endeavoring after greater degrees of it and practicing every day acts of humility as you every day practice acts of devotion.

You would not imagine yourself to be devout because in your judgment you approved of prayers and often declared your mind in favor of devotion. Yet how many people imagine themselves humble for no other reason than they often commend humility and make vehement declarations against pride!

Caecus is a rich man, of good breeding and very fine parts. He is haughty and imperious to all his inferiors, is very full of everything that he says or does, and never imagines it possible for such a judgment as his to be mistaken. He changes everything in his house and his habit as often as anything more elegant comes in his way. Caecus would have been very religious, but that he always thought he was so.

There is nothing so odious to Caecus as a proud man. The misfortune is that he is so very quick-sighted that he discovers in almost everybody some strokes of vanity. On the other hand, he is exceedingly fond of humble and modest persons. Humility, he says, is so amiable a quality that it forces our esteem wherever we meet with it.

Caecus no more suspects himself to be proud than he suspects his lack of sense. And the reason of it is that he always finds himself so in love with humility and so enraged at pride.

It is very true, Caecus, that you love humility and abhor pride. You are no hypocrite. But then take this along with you, Caecus, that you love humility and hate pride only in other people. You never once in your life thought of any other pride than that which you have seen in other people.

The case of Caecus is a common case. Many people live in pride and yet never suspect themselves to be governed by pride because they know how much they dislike proud people. They know how mightily they are pleased with humility and modesty wherever they find them. The fuller of pride anyone is himself, the more impatient will he be at the smallest instances of it in other people.

You must, therefore, act by a quite contrary measure and reckon yourself humble only so far as you impose every instance of humility upon yourself and never call for it in other people — so far an enemy to pride that you never spare it in yourself or censure it in other persons.

Now, in order to do this you need only consider that pride

and humility signify nothing to you except so far as they are your own. The loving of humility, therefore, is of no benefit to you except as you love to see all your own thoughts, words, and actions governed by it. And the hating of pride does you no good except as you hate to harbor any degree of it in your own heart.

Now in order to begin in the practice of humility you must take it for granted that you are proud. You should believe also that pride is your greatest weakness, that your heart is most subject to it, that it is constantly stealing upon you. This is what most people, especially beginners in a pious life, may with great truth think of themselves. For there is no one vice that is more deeply rooted in our nature or that receives such constant nourishment from almost everything that we think or do.

If, therefore, you find it disagreeable to entertain this opinion of yourself, you may be assured, as if an angel from heaven had told you, that you have not only much but all of your humility to seek. For you can have no greater sign of a confirmed pride than when you think that you are humble enough. He who thinks he loves God enough shows himself to be an entire stranger to the holy passion. So! He who thinks he has humility enough shows that he is not so much as a beginner in the practice of true humility.

Chapter XVII

The Practice of Humility

Every person who applies himself to the exercise of this
virtue of humility must, as I said before, consider himself
as a learner of something that is contrary to former habits of
mind and that can be obtained only by daily and constant
practice.

He not only has as much to do as he who learns some new
art or science, but he also has a great deal to unlearn. According to the spirit and vogue of this world, whose corrupt air we
have all breathed, there are many things that pass for great and
honorable that are so far from being so that the true greatness
and honor of our nature consists in the not desiring of them.

To abound in wealth, to have fine houses and rich clothes,
to be attended with splendor and equipage, to be beautiful in
our persons, to have titles of dignity, to be above our fellow
creatures, to be looked on with admiration, to overcome our
enemies with power, to subdue all who oppose us, to set ourselves in as much splendor as we can, to live highly and magnificently, to eat and drink and delight ourselves in the most
costly manner — these are the great, the honorable, the desirable things to which the spirit of the world turns the eyes of
all people. And many a man is afraid of not engaging in the
pursuit of these things lest the same world should take him for
a fool.

The history of the gospel is chiefly the history of Christ's conquest over the spirit of the world. And the number of true Christians is only the number of those who, following the spirit of Christ, have lived contrary to this spirit of the world. " If any man has not the Spirit of Christ, he is none of his." Again, " Whatsoever is born of God overcometh the world." " Set your affection on things above, not on things on the earth. For ye are dead, and your life is hid with Christ in God." This is the language of the whole New Testament. This is the mark of Christianity. You are to die to the spirit and temper of the world and live a new life in the spirit of Jesus Christ. How many people swell with pride and vanity for such things as they would not know how to value at all, but that they are admired in the world! How often would a man have yielded to the haughtiness and ill nature of others, and shown a submissive temper, but that he dares not pass for such a poor-spirited man in the opinion of the world! Many a man would often drop a resentment and forgive an affront, but that he is afraid the world would not forgive him. How many would practice Christian temperance and sobriety in its utmost perfection, were it not for the censure which the world passes upon such a life! Thus do the impressions that we have received from living in the world enslave our minds. We dare not attempt to be eminent in the sight of God for fear of being little in the eyes of the world.

From this quarter arises the greatest difficulty of humility. It cannot subsist in any mind except so far as it is dead to the world and has parted with all desires of enjoying its greatness and honors. In order to be truly humble you must unlearn all those notions which you have been all your life learning from this corrupt spirit of the world. But great as the power of the world is, it is all built upon a blind obedience. We need only open our eyes to get quit of its power. Ask whom you will, learned or unlearned — everyone seems to know and confess that the general spirit of the world is nothing else but humor, folly, and extravagance.

Again: to lessen your fear and regard for the opinion of the world, think how soon the world will disregard you and have no more thought or concern about you than about the poorest animal that died in a ditch. Your friends, if they can, may bury you with some distinction and set up a monument to let posterity see that your dust lies under such a stone. When that is done, all is done. Your place is filled up by another. The world is just in the same state it was. You are blotted out of sight, and as much forgotten by the world as if you had never belonged to it. Is it therefore worth your while to lose the smallest degree of virtue, for the sake of pleasing so bad a master, and so false a friend, as the world is?

Lastly, you must consider what behavior the profession of Christianity requires of you with regard to the world. This is plainly delivered in these words: " Who gave himself for our sins, that he might deliver us from this present evil world." Christianity implies a deliverance from this world, and he who professes it professes to live contrary to everything that is peculiar to this evil world.

Our blessed Lord himself has fully determined this point in these words: " They are not of the world, even as I am not of the world." This is the state of Christianity with regard to this world. If you are not thus out of and contrary to the world, you lack the distinguishing mark of Christianity. You do not belong to Christ except by being out of the world as he was out of it. We may deceive ourselves with vain and softening comments upon these words, but they are understood in their first simplicity and plainness by everyone who reads them in the same spirit that our blessed Lord spoke them.

The Christian's great conquest over the world is all contained in the mystery of Christ upon the cross. Thus was the cross of Christ in Saint Paul's days the glory of Christians — not because it signified their not being ashamed to own a Master who was crucified, but because it signified their glorying in a religion that was nothing else but a doctrine of the cross. The cross called them to the same suffering spirit, the same sacrifice of themselves, the same renunciation of the world, the same humility and meekness, the same patient bearing of injuries, reproaches, and contempts, and the same dying to all the greatness, honors, and happiness of this world that Christ showed upon the cross. To have a true idea of Christianity we must not consider our blessed Lord as suffering in our stead, but as our Representative, acting in our name, and with such particular merit as to make our joining with him acceptable unto God.

The necessity of this conformity to all that Christ did and suffered upon our account is very plain from the whole tenor of Scripture:

First, As to his sufferings: This is the only condition of our being saved by them: If we suffer with him, we shall also reign with him.

Secondly, As to his crucifixion: Knowing this, that our old self is crucified with him. Here you see Christ is not crucified in our stead, but unless our old self be really crucified with him, the cross of Christ will profit us nothing.

Thirdly, As to the death of Christ, the condition is this: If we be dead with him, we believe that we shall also live with him. If therefore Christ be dead alone, if we are not dead with him, we shall not live with him.

Finally, As to the resurrection of Christ, the Scripture shows us how we are to partake of the benefit of it: If ye be risen with Christ, seek those things which are above, where Christ sitteth on the right hand of God.

Thus you see how plainly the Scriptures set forth our blessed Lord as our Representative, acting and suffering in our name, binding and obliging us to conform to all that he did and suffered for us.

Had you lived with our Saviour as his true disciple, you had then been hated as he was. And if you live in his spirit the world will be the same enemy to you now that it was to him then. " If you were of the world," saith our blessed Lord, " the world would love its own: but because ye are not of the world, but I have chosen you out of the world, therefore the world hateth you." We are apt to lose the true meaning of these words by considering them only as a historical description of something that was the state of our Saviour and his disciples at that time. But this is reading the Scriptures as a dead letter. They as exactly describe the state of true Christians at this time and at all other times to the end of the world.

You will perhaps say that the world has now become Christian, at least that part of it where we live, and therefore the world is not now to be considered in that state of opposition to Christianity. It is granted that the world now professes Christianity. But will anyone say that this Christian world is of the Spirit of Christ? Are its general tempers the tempers of Christ? Are the passions of sensuality, self-love, pride, covetousness, ambition, and vainglory less contrary to the spirit of the gospel now that they are among Christians than when they were among pagans?

So far from considering the world as in a state of less opposition to Christianity than in the first times of the gospel, we must guard against it as a greater and more dangerous enemy. It is a greater enemy because it has greater power over Christians by its favors, riches, honors, rewards, and protection than it had by the fire and fury of its persecutions. It is a more dangerous enemy by having lost its appearance of enmity. Because outward profession of Christianity makes it no longer considered as an enemy, the generality of people are easily persuaded to resign themselves up to be governed and directed by it.

Christians had nothing to fear from the pagan world but the loss of their lives. But the world become a friend makes it difficult for them to save their religion. While pride, sensuality, covetousness, and ambition had only the authority of the pagan world, Christians were thereby made more intent upon the contrary virtues. But when pride, sensuality, covetousness, and ambition have the authority of the Christian world, then private Christians are in the utmost danger — not only of being shamed out of the practice but of losing the very notion of the piety of the gospel.

These reflections will, I hope, help you to break through those difficulties and resist those temptations which the authority and fashion of the world have raised against the practice of Christian humility.

Chapter XVIII

The Spirit of a Better Education

A NOTHER DIFFICULTY in the practice of humility arises from our education. For the most part, we are all of us corruptly educated and then committed to take our place in a corrupt world. It is no wonder, then, if examples of great piety are so seldom seen. Great parts of the world are undone by being born and bred in families that have no religion — where they are made vicious and irregular by being like those with whom they first lived. But this is not the thing I now mean. The education that I here intend is such as children generally receive from virtuous and sober parents, and learned tutors and governors.

Had we continued perfect as God created the first man, perhaps the perfection of our nature had been a sufficient self-instruction for everyone. But as sickness and disease have created the necessity of medicines and physicians, so the change and disorder of our rational nature have introduced the necessity of education and tutors. And as the only end of the physician is to restore nature to its own state, so the only end of education is to restore our rational nature to its proper state. Education, therefore, is to be considered as a reason borrowed at second hand which is to supply, as far as it can, the loss of original perfection. And as medicine may justly be called the art of restoring health, so education should be considered in no other light than as the art of recovering to man the use of his reason.

Now as the instruction of every art or science is founded upon the discoveries, wisdom, experience, and maxims of the several great men who have labored in it, so human wisdom or the right use of our reason to which young people should be called by their education is nothing else but the best experience and finest reasonings of men who have devoted themselves to the study of wisdom and the improvement of human nature.

Paternus lived about two hundred years ago. He had but one son, whom he educated himself in his own house. As they were sitting together in the garden when the child was ten years old Paternus thus began:

"The little time you have been in the world, my child, you have spent wholly with me. My love and tenderness to you has made you look upon me as your only friend and benefactor, and the cause of all the comfort and pleasure which you enjoy. Your heart, I know, would be ready to break with grief if you thought this was the last day that I should live with you.

"But, my child, though you now think yourself mighty happy because you have hold of my hand, you are now in the hands and under the tender care of a much greater Father and Friend than I am. His love to you is far greater than mine, and from him you receive such blessings as no mortal can give.

"You see, my son, this wide and large firmament over our heads, where the sun and moon and all the stars appear in their turn. If you were to be carried up to any of these bodies at this vast distance from us, you would still discover others as much above you as the stars you see now are above the earth. Were you to go up or down, east or west, north or south, you would find the same height without any top and the same depth without any bottom.

"And yet, my child, so great is God that all these bodies added together are but as a grain of sand in his sight. Yet you are as much the care of this great God and Father of all worlds and all spirits as if he had no son but you, or as if there were no creature for him to love and protect but you alone. He numbers the hairs of your head, watches over you, sleeping and waking, and has preserved you from a thousand dangers, which neither you nor I know anything of.

"Therefore, my child, fear and worship and love God. Your eyes, indeed, cannot see him. But all things that you see are so many marks of his power and presence, and he is nearer to you than anything that you can see. Take him for your Lord and Father and Friend. Look up unto him as the Fountain and Cause of all the good that you have received through my hands. Reverence me only as the bearer and minister of God's good things unto you. And he, who blessed my father before I was born, will bless you when I am dead.

"God, my child, is all love and wisdom and goodness. Everything that he has made and every action that he does is the effect of them all. Therefore you cannot please God except as you strive to walk in love, wisdom, and goodness. As all wisdom, love, and goodness proceed from God, so nothing but love, wisdom, and goodness can lead to God. When you love that which God loves, you act with him, you join yourself to him. When you love what he dislikes, then you oppose him and separate yourself from him. This is the true and right way: Think what God loves and love it with all your heart.

"First of all, my child, worship and adore God. Think of him magnificently. Speak of him reverently. Magnify his providence. Adore his power. Frequent his service. And pray unto him frequently and constantly.

"Next to this, love your neighbor — who is all mankind — with such tenderness and affection as you love yourself. Think how God loves all mankind; how merciful he is to them; how tender he is of them; how carefully he preserves them. And then strive to love the world as God loves it.

"God would have all men to be happy. Therefore, will and desire the same. All men are great instances of divine love. Therefore, let all men be instances of your love.

"But above all, my son, mark this: Never do anything through strife, or envy, or emulation, or vainglory. Never do anything in order to excel other people, but in order to please God and because it is his will that you should do everything in the best manner that you can. For if it is once a pleasure to you to excel other people, it will by degrees be a pleasure to you to see other people not so good as yourself. Banish, therefore, every thought of self-pride and self-distinction, and accustom yourself to rejoice in all the excellencies and perfections of your fellow creatures. Be as glad to see any of their good actions as your own.

"The time of practicing these precepts, my child, will soon be over with you. The world will soon slip through your hands. Rather, you will soon slip through it. It seems but the other day since I received these same instructions from my dear father. And the God who gave me ears to hear and a heart to receive what my father said unto me will, I hope, give you grace to love and follow the same instructions."

Thus did Paternus educate his son.

CHAPTER XIX

On Educating Our Daughters

THE EDUCATION of daughters makes it exceeding difficult for them to understand and practice humility as the spirit of Christianity requires. The right education of women is of utmost importance to human life. There is nothing more desirable for the common good of all the world. For though women do not carry on the trade and business of the world, yet as mother who have the care of their children they are entrusted with that which is of the greatest consequence to human life. For this reason, good or bad women are likely to do as much good or harm in the world as good or bad men in the greatest business of life.

As the strength or weakness of our bodies results largely from the methods of treatment when we were young, so the soundness or folly of our minds results no less from those examples and ways of thinking which we eagerly receive from the love, tenderness, authority, and constant conduct of our mothers. As we call our first language our mother tongue, so we may as justly call our first attitudes our mother attitudes. Perhaps it may be found more easy to forget the language than to part entirely with those attitudes which we learned in the nursery.

It is therefore much to be lamented that the members of this sex on whom depends the first forming both of our bodies and our minds are so often educated in pride and useless endeavors. They are not suffered to compete with us in the arts and sciences of learning and eloquence, in which I have much suspicion they would often prove our superiors. But we turn them over to the study of beauty and dress, and the whole world conspires to make them think of nothing else. Fathers and mothers, friends and relations, seem to have no other wish toward a little girl but that she may have a fair skin, a fine shape, dress well, and dance to admiration.

This matter is still more to be lamented because when women are spoiled we spoil that part of the world which would otherwise furnish the best examples of a devout life. For I believe it may be said that for the most part there is a finer sense, a clearer mind, a readier apprehension, and gentler dispositions among the women than among the generality of men.

Matilda is a fine woman of good background, great sense, and much religion. She has three daughters who were educated by herself. She will not trust them with anyone else or at any school for fear they should learn something wrong. She had them read the Scriptures so often that they can repeat great parts by memory, and there is scarce a good book of devotion but you may find it on their shelves.

But Matilda was born in corrupt times and she lacks examples of Christian perfection. She has hardly seen a piety higher than her own, so she has many defects — and communicates them all to her daughters. Her daughters see her great zeal for religion, but then they see an equal earnestness for all sorts of finery. They see she is not negligent of her devotions, but then they see her more careful to preserve her complexion and to prevent those changes which time and age threaten. They are afraid to meet her if they have missed church, but they are more afraid to see her if they are not laced as strait as they can possibly be.

Matilda is so intent upon all the arts of improving their dress that the maid is often forced to dress and undress her daughters three or four times in a day before she is satisfied. She stints them in their meals and tells them how many fine shapes she has seen spoiled in her time for lack of such care. If a pimple rises in their faces she is greatly disturbed, and they are as afraid for her to see it as if they had committed some great sin. Whenever they begin to look too sanguine and healthful, she calls in the assistance of the doctor, and if physic or issues will keep the complexion from becoming too coarse or ruddy she thinks them well employed.

The eldest daughter lived as long as she could under this discipline and died in the twentieth year of her age. Her youngest daughter has run away with a gamester, a handsome man who has no superior in dressing and dancing. Matilda says she would die with grief but that her conscience tells her she has contributed no cause. She points out their many books of devotion to testify what care she has taken to establish her children in a life of solid piety and devotion.

Now, though many daughters are reared in a better way than this, yet I believe that many more are not brought up so well or accustomed to so much religion as in the present instance. Some people who judge hastily will perhaps here say that I am exercising too great a severity against the women. But more discerning persons will observe that I entirely spare the sex and only condemn that education which is so injurious to their welfare and which deprives them of the benefit of their excellent natures.

How possible it is to bring up daughters in the more excellent way, let the following character declare: Eusebia is a pious widow, well-born and well-bred, and has a good estate for five daughters, whom she brings up as one entrusted by God to rear five children for the Kingdom. She, her daughters, and her maids meet together at the hours of prayer and spend the rest of their time in such good works and innocent diversions as render them fit to return to their psalms and prayers. She has divided part of her estate among them that each one may be charitable out of her portion.

Eusebia teaches them in all kinds of activities that are proper for women — such as sewing, knitting, spinning — not for their amusement, but that they may be serviceable to themselves and others. She tells them she had rather see them reduced to the necessity of maintaining themselves than to have riches to excuse them from labor.

If Eusebia has lived as free from sin as it is possible for human nature, it is because she is always guarding against all instances of pride. And if her virtues are stronger and higher than others, it is because they are all founded in a deep humility.

" My children," says she, " when your father died I was much pitied for having all the care of a family and the management of an estate. But my own grief was founded upon another principle: I was grieved to see myself deprived of so faithful a friend, and that such an eminent example of Christian virtues should be taken from the eyes of his children before they were of an age to love and follow.

" For though you were all born of my body and bear your father's name, yet you are pure spirits. I do not mean that you have not bodies that want meat and drink, sleep and clothing. But all that deserves to be called 'you' is nothing else but spirit — a being spiritual and rational in its natures that is as contrary to all fleshly beings as life is contrary to death; that is made in the image of God to live forever, to enjoy life, reason, knowledge, and happiness in the presence of God to all eternity. Everything that you call yours, besides this spirit, is but like your clothing — something that is to be used for a while and then to signify no more to you than the clothing and bodies of other people.

" But, my children, you are not only spirits, but you are fallen spirits. You began your life in a state of disorder, full of passions that blind and darken the reason of your mind and incline you to that which is hurtful. Your bodies are not only poor and perishing like your clothes, but they are like infected clothes which fill you with ill diseases and moods, which oppress the soul with sickly appetites and vain cravings.

" All of us are like two beings who have, as it were, two hearts within us: with the one we see, taste, and admire reason, purity, and holiness: with the other we incline to pride, vanity, and sensual delights. This internal war we always feel more or less. If you would know the one thing necessary, it is this: to preserve and perfect all that is rational, holy, and divine in our nature, and to mortify, remove, and destroy all that is vain, prideful, and sensual in our nature.

" While you live thus, you live like yourselves. Whenever you have less regard to your souls or more regard to your bodies, whenever you are more intent upon adorning your persons than upon perfecting your souls, you are much more beside yourselves than he who would rather have a laced coat than a healthful body.

" You know, my children, the high perfection and the great rewards of virginity. You know how it frees from worldly cares and troubles and furnishes means and opportunities of higher advancements in a divine life. Therefore, love and esteem and honor virginity. Bless God for all that glorious company of holy virgins who from the beginning of Christianity have renounced the cares and pleasures of matrimony to be perpetual examples of solitude, contemplation, and prayer.

" But as everyone has his proper gift from God, as I look upon you all to be so many great blessings of a married state, so I leave it to your choice. Either do as I have done or aspire after higher degrees of perfection in a virgin state of life. I desire nothing, I press nothing upon you, but to make the most of human life and to aspire after perfection in whatever state of life you choose.

" Whether married, therefore, or unmarried, consider yourselves as mothers and sisters, as friends and relations, to all who need your assistance. Never allow yourselves to be idle while others are in want of anything your hands can make for them. This useful, charitable, humble, employment of yourselves is what I recommend to you with great earnestness as being a substantial part of a wise and pious life. And besides the good you will thereby do to other people, every virtue of your own heart will be very much improved by it. For next to reading, meditation, and prayer, there is nothing that so secures our hearts from foolish passions, nothing that preserves so holy and wise a frame of mind, as some useful, humble employment of ourselves.

" The humility of this employment will be as beneficial to you as the charity of it. It will keep you from all vain and proud thoughts of your own state and distinction in life, and from treating the poor as creatures of a different species. By accustoming yourselves to this labor and service for the poor, as the representatives of Jesus Christ, you will soon find your heart softened into the greatest meekness and lowliness toward them. You will reverence their state and condition, think it an honor to serve them, and never be so pleased with yourself as when you are most humbly employed in their service. This will make you true disciples of your meek Lord and Master, who came into the world not to be ministered unto but to minister, and, though he was Lord of all, and among the creatures of his own making, yet was among them as one who serves.

" Though you intend to marry, yet let the time never come till you find a man who has those perfections which you have been laboring after yourselves — who is likely to be a friend to all your virtues and with whom it is better to live than to lack the benefit of his example.

" Never allow yourselves to despise those who do not follow your rules of life, but force your hearts to love and pray for them. Let humility be always whispering into your ears that you yourselves would fall from those rules tomorrow if God should leave you to your own strength and wisdom.

" Think, therefore, my children, that the soul of your good father, who is now with God, speaks to you through my mouth. Let the double desire of your father, who is gone, and of me, who am with you, prevail upon you to love God, to study your own perfection, to practice humility, and with innocent labor and charity to do all the good that you can to all your fellow creatures, till God calls you to another life."

Thus did the pious widow educate her daughters. The spirit of this education speaks so plainly for itself that I hope I need say nothing in its justification.

CHAPTER XX

Intercession as an
Act of Universal Love

IT WILL perhaps be thought by some people that these hours of prayer come too thick; that they can only be observed by people of great leisure and ought not to be pressed upon the generality of men who have the cares of families, trades, and employments; and that they are fitting only for monasteries and nunneries. To this it is answered, first, that this method of devotion is not pressed upon any sort of people as absolutely necessary, but recommended to all people as the best, the happiest, and most perfect way of life. If a great and exemplary devotion is as much the greatest happiness and perfection of a merchant, a soldier, or a man of quality as it is the greatest happiness and perfection of the most retired contemplative life, then it is proper to recommend it without any abatements to one order of men as to another. Happiness and perfection are of the same worth and value to all people.

The gentlemen and tradesmen may, and must, spend much of their time differently from the pious monk in the cloister or the contemplative hermit in the desert. But then as the monk and hermit lose the ends of retirement unless they make it all serviceable to devotion, so the gentlemen and merchant fail of the greatest ends of a social life, and live to their loss in the world, unless devotion be their chief and governing temper.

Unless gentlemen can show that they have another God than
the Father of our Lord Jesus Chirst, it is in vain to plead their
state, dignity, and pleasures as reasons for not preparing their
souls for God by a strict and regular devotion. If a merchant
having forborne from too great business that he might quietly
attend on the service of God should, therefore, die worth twenty
instead of fifty thousand pounds, could anyone say that he had
mistaken his calling or gone a loser out of the world? I cannot
see why every gentleman, merchant, or soldier should not put
those questions seriously to himself.

What is the best thing for me to intend and drive at in all
my actions? What shall I do to make the most of human life?
What ways shall I wish that I had taken when I am leaving the
world? Now here is desired no more devotion in anyone's life
than the answering that these few questions require.

Any devotion that is not the greater advantage of him who
uses it than anything that he can do in place of it — any devotion that does not procure an infinitely greater good than can
be got by neglecting it — is freely yielded up. But if people will
live in so much ignorance as never to put these questions to
themselves, but push on a blind life at all chances in quest of
they know not what, nor why — without considering what
God, reason, eternity, and their own happiness require of them
— it is for the honor of devotion that none can neglect it but
those who are thus inconsiderate and who dare not inquire
after that which is the best and most worthy of their choice.
For people, therefore, of figure, or business, or dignity in the
world to leave great piety and eminent devotion to any particular orders of men, or such as they think have little else to
do in the world, is to leave the Kingdom of God to them. For
it is the very end of Christianity to redeem all orders of men

into one holy society — that rich and poor, high and low, masters and servants, may in one and the same spirit of piety become " a chosen generation, a royal priesthood, a holy nation, a peculiar people," who are to show forth the praises of him who hath called them " out of darkness into his marvelous light."

Thus much being said to show that great devotion and holiness are not being left to any particular sort of people, but are to be the common spirit of all who desire to live up to the terms of common Christianity, I now proceed to consider the nature and necessity of universal love, which is here recommended to be the subject of your devotion at the twelve o'clock hour. You are here also called to *intercession* as the most proper exercise to raise and preserve that love.

By intercession is meant a praying to God and interceding with him for our fellow creatures. Our blessed Lord hath recommended his love to us as the pattern and example of our love to one another. As, therefore, he is continually making intercession for us all, so ought we to intercede and pray for one another. " A new commandment," said he, " I give unto you, That ye love one another, as I have loved you. By this shall all men know that ye are my disciples, if ye love one another." The newness of this precept did not consist in the idea that men were commanded to love one another. This was an old precept, both of the law of Moses and of nature. But it was new in this respect: that it was to imitate a new and till then unheard-of example of love. It was to love one another as Christ had loved us. And if men are to know that we are disciples of Christ by thus loving one another according to his new example of love, then it is certain that if we are void of this love we make it as plainly known unto men that we are none of his disciples.

There is no principle of the heart that is more acceptable to God than a universal fervent love to all mankind, wishing and praying for their happiness — because there is no principle of the heart that makes us more like God, who is love and goodness itself and created all beings for their enjoyment of happiness.

The greatest idea that we can frame of God is when we conceive him to be a Being of infinite love and goodness, using an infinite wisdom and power for the common good and happiness of all his creatures. The highest notion, therefore, that we can form of man is when we conceive him as like to God in this respect as he can be — using all his infinite faculties, whether wisdom, power, or prayers, for the common good of all his fellow creatures.

If, therefore, we desire this divine virtue of love, we must exercise and practice our hearts in the love of all, because it is not *Christian* love till it is the love of all. If a man could keep this whole law of love and yet offend in one point, he would be guilty of all. For as one allowed instance of injustice destroys the justice of all our other actions, so one allowed instance of envy, spite, and ill-will renders all our other acts of benevolence and affection worth nothing. Acts of love that proceed not from a principle of universal love are but like acts of justice that proceed from a heart not disposed to universal justice.

Now the noblest motive to this universal tenderness and affection is founded in this doctrine: " God is love; and he that dwelleth in love dwelleth in God."

Who, therefore, whose heart has any tendency toward God, would not aspire after this divine quality which so changes and exalts our nature into a union with him? How should we re-

joice in the exercise and practice of this love which is an assurance to us that God is in us! But we must observe that love
only has this mighty power of uniting us to God when it is so
pure and universal as to imitate that love which God beareth
to all his creatures. As God forgives all and gives grace to all, so
we should forgive all those injuries and affronts which we receive from others, and do all the good that we can to them.

Our power of doing external acts of love and goodness is
often very narrow and restrained. There are, it may be, but few
people to whom we can contribute any worldly relief. But
through our outward means of doing good are often thus
limited, yet if our hearts are but full of love and goodness, we
get, as it were, an infinite power. God will attribute to us those
good words, those acts of love and tender charities, which we
sincerely desired and would gladly have performed had it been
in our power.

You cannot heal all the sick or relieve all the poor. You cannot comfort all in distress nor be a father to all the fatherless.
You cannot, it may be, deliver many from their misfortunes or
teach them to find comfort in God. But if there is a love and
tenderness in your heart that delights in these good works and
excites you to do all that you can — if your love has no bounds
but continually wishes and prays for the relief and happiness
of all who are in distress — you will be received by God as a
benefactor to those who have had nothing from you but your
good will and tender affections.

The love of our neighbor is only a branch of our love to
God. For when we love God with all our hearts, and with all
our souls, and with all our strength, we shall necessarily love
those beings who are so nearly related to God, who have everything from him, and who are created by him to be objects of

his own eternal love. If I hate or despise any one man in the world, I hate something that God cannot hate, and despise that which he loves. Can I think that I love God with all my heart while I hate that which belongs only to God, which has no other master but him, which bears his image, which is part of his family, and which exists only by the continuance of his love toward it? It was the impossibility of this that made Saint John say that if any man says he loves God, and hates his brother, he is a liar.

These reasons sufficiently show us that no love is holy or religious till it becomes universal.

As it was the sins of the world that made the Son of God become a compassionate suffering Advocate for all mankind, so no one is of the spirit of Christ but he who has the utmost compassion for sinners. Nor is there any greater sign of your own perfection than when you find yourself all love and compassion toward those who are very weak and defective. And on the other hand, you have never less reason to be pleased with yourself than when you find yourself most angry and offended at the behaviour of others. All sin is certainly to be hated and abhorred, wherever it is. But then we must set ourselves against sin as we do against sickness and diseases: by showing ourselves tender and compassionate to the sick and diseased. All hatred of sin that does not fill the heart with the softest, tenderest affections toward persons miserable in it is the servant of sin at the same time that it seems to be hating it.

There is no temper which good men ought more carefully to watch and guard against than this. It is a temper that lurks and hides itself under the cover of many virtues and, by being unsuspected, does the more mischief. A man naturally fancies that it is his own exceeding love of virtue that makes him not able to bear with those who lack it. When he abhors one man, despises another, and cannot bear the name of a third, he supposes it all to be a proof of his own high sense of virtue and hatred of sin. But if this had been the spirit of the Son of God, if he had hated sin in this manner, there would have been no redemption of the world. If God had hated sinners in this manner, day and night, the world itself would have ceased long ago.

God loves us — not because we are wise and good and holy — but in pity to us, because we lack this happiness. He loves us in order to make us good. Our love, therefore, must take this same course — not looking for or requiring the merit of our brethren, but pitying their disorders and wishing them all the good that they lack and are capable of receiving. When, therefore, you let loose any ill-natured passion, either of hatred or contempt, toward (as you suppose) an ill man, consider what you would think of another that was doing the same toward a good man and be assured that you are committing the same sin.

You will perhaps say, " How is it possible to love a good and a bad man in the same degree? " Just as it is possible to be as just and faithful to a good man as to an evil man. Are you in any difficulty about performing justice and faithfulness to a bad man? Are you in any doubts whether you need be so just and faithful to him as you need be to a good man? Now why is it that you are in no doubt about it? It is because you know that justice and faithfulness are founded upon reasons that never vary or change, that have no dependence upon the merits of men, but are founded in the nature of things, in the laws of God, and therefore are to be observed with an equal exactness toward good and bad men. Do but think thus justly of charity or love to your neighbor — that it is founded upon reasons that vary not, that have no dependence upon the merits of men — and then you will find it as possible to perform the same exact charity to all men, whether good or bad. The whole of the matter is this: The actions that you are to love, esteem, and admire are the actions of good and pious men; but the persons to whom you are to do all the good you can are *all* persons, whether good or bad.

Again, if you think it hardly possible to dislike the actions of unreasonable men and yet have a true love for them, consider this with relation to yourself. It is very possible, I hope, for you not only to dislike but to detest and abhor a great many of your own past actions and to accuse yourself of great folly for them. But do you then lose any of those tender sentiments toward yourself which you used to have? Do you cease to wish well to yourself? Is not the love of yourself as strong as at any other time? Now what is thus possible with relation to ourselves is in the same manner possible with relation to others. We may have the highest good wishes toward them, desiring for them every good that we desire for ourselves, and at the same time dislike their way of life.

But now, if the lack of a true and exact charity be so great a lack that, as Saint Paul saith, it renders our greatest virtues but empty sounds and tinkling cymbals, how highly does it concern us to study every art and practice every method of raising our souls to this state of charity! It is for this reason that you are here desired not to let this hour of prayer pass without a full and solemn supplication to God for all the instances of a universal love and benevolence to all mankind. Such daily constant devotion is the only likely means of preserving you in such a state of love as is necessary to prove you to be a true follower of Jesus Christ.

CHAPTER XXI

On the Advantages of Intercession

THAT INTERCESSION is a great and necessary part of Christian devotion is very evident from Scripture. The first followers of Christ seem to support all their love and to maintain all their intercourse and correspondence by mutual prayers for one another. Saint Paul, whether he writes to churches or particular persons, shows his intercession to be perpetual. This was the ancient friendship of Christians, uniting and cementing their hearts. And when the same spirit of intercession is again in the world — when Christianity has the same power over the hearts of people that it then had — this holy friendship will be again in fashion and Christians will be again the wonder of the world.

Be daily, therefore, on your knees praying for others in such forms, with such length, importunity, and earnestness as you use for yourself. You will then find that all little, ill-natured passions die away and your heart will grow great and generous. When our intercession is made an exercise of love and care for those among whom our lot is fallen, or who belong to us in a nearer relation, it becomes the greatest benefit to ourselves and produces its best effects in our own hearts. For there is nothing that makes us love a man so much as praying for him. When you can once do this sincerely for any man, you have fitted your soul for the performance of everything that is kind and civil toward him. By considering yourself as an advocate with God for your neighbors and acquaintances you would never find it hard to be at peace with them yourself.

Ouranius is a holy priest, full of the spirit of the gospel, watching, laboring, and praying for a poor country village. Every soul in it is as dear to him as himself. And he loves them all as he loves himself because he prays for them all as often as he prays for himself. He goes about his parish and visits everybody in it to encourage their virtues, to assist them with his advice and counsel, to discover their manner of life, and to know the state of their souls — all that he may intercede with God for them according to their particular necessities.

The rudeness, ill nature, or perverse behavior of any of his flock used to betray him into impatience, but it now raises no other passion in him than a desire of being upon his knees in prayer to God for them. Thus have his prayers for others altered and amended the state of his own heart. This devotion softens his heart, enlightens his mind, sweetens his temper, and makes everything that comes from him instructive, amiable, and affecting.

Ouranius is mightily affected with this passage of holy Scripture: " The effectual fervent prayer of a righteous man availeth much." This makes him practice all the arts of holy living and aspire after every instance of piety and righteousness that his prayers for his flock may have their full force and avail much with God. Such are the happy effects that a devout intercession has produced in the life of Ouranius. And if other people were to imitate this example, in such a manner as suited their particular state of life, they would certainly find the same happy effects.

If masters, for instance, were thus to remember their servants in their prayers, beseeching God to bless them and suiting their petitions to the particular wants and necessities of their servants, the benefit would be as great to themselves as to their servants. This devotion would give them another spirit and make them consider how to make proper returns of care, kindness, and protection to those who had spent their strength and time in service and attendance upon them. And if gentlemen think it too low an employment for their state and dignity to exercise such a devotion as this for their servants, let them consider how far they are from the spirit of Christ.

Again, if parents should make themselves advocates and intercessors with God for their children, constantly applying to heaven in behalf of them, nothing would be more likely not only to bless their children but also to form and dispose their own minds to the performance of everything excellent and praiseworthy. If parents should be daily calling upon God in a solemn, deliberate manner, altering and extending their intercessions as the state and growth of their children required, such devotion would make them very circumspect in the government of themselves lest their example should hinder that which they so constantly desired in their prayers. How tenderly, how religiously would such a father converse with his children! How fearful would he be of all greedy and unjust ways of raising their fortune, lest he should thereby render them incapable of those graces which he was so often beseeching God to grant them!

Lastly, all people, when they feel the first approaches of resentment, envy, or contempt toward others, should have recourse to a particular and extraordinary intercession with God for such persons as have raised their envy, resentment, or discontent. This would be a certain way to prevent the growth of all uncharitable tempers, for you cannot possibly despise and ridicule one whom your private prayers recommend to the love and favor of God. For to despise one for whom Christ dies is to be as contrary to Christ as to despise anything that Christ has said or done.

But to return: intercession is not only the best arbitrator of all differences, the best promoter of true friendship, the best cure and preservative against all unkind tempers, all angry and haughty passions; it is also of great use to discover to us the true state of our own hearts.

Susurrus is a pious, temperate, good man, remarkable for an abundance of excellent qualities. Yet Susurrus had a prodigious failing along with these virtues. He had a mighty inclination to hear and discover all the defects and infirmities of those about him. If you would but whisper anything gently, Susurrus was ready to receive it.

Susurrus once whispered to a particular friend in great secrecy something too bad to be spoken publicly. His friend made him this reply: " You say, Susurrus, that you are glad it has not yet taken wind, and that you have some hopes it may not prove true. Go home, therefore, to your closet and pray to God for this man in such manner and with such earnestness as you would pray for yourself on the like occasion."

Susurrus was exceedingly affected by this rebuke and felt the force of it upon his conscience in as lively a manner as if he had seen the books opened at the Day of Judgment. From that time to this he has constantly disciplined himself to this method of intercession. His heart is so entirely changed by it that he can now no more privately whisper anything to the injury of another than he can openly pray to God to do people hurt.

I have laid before you the many and great advantages of intercession. You have seen what a divine friendship it begets among Christians; how dear it renders all relations and neighbors to one another; how it tends to make clergymen, masters, and parents exemplary and perfect in all their duties; how certainly it destroys all envy, spite, and ill-natured passions; how speedily it reconciles all differences; and with what a piercing light it discovers to a man the true state of his heart. These considerations will, I hope, persuade you to make such intercession as is proper for your state.

CHAPTER XXII

The Nature and Duty of Conformity
to the Will of God

I HAVE RECOMMENDED certain subjects to be made the fixed
and chief matter of your devotion at all the hours of prayer
which have been already considered: thanksgiving and oblation
of yourself to God at your first prayers in the morning; the
great virtue of Christian humility at nine; and all the graces of
universal love at twelve.

Now at the third hour of the afternoon you are desired to
consider the necessity of resignation and conformity to the will
of God, and to make this great virtue the principal matter of
your prayers.

There is nothing wise, or holy, or just, but the great will of
God. This is as strictly true, in the most rigid sense, as to say
that nothing is infinite and eternal but God. No beings, therefore, whether in heaven or on earth, can be wise, or holy, or
just but in so far as they conform to this will of God. It is conformity to this will that gives virtue and perfection to the
highest services of the angels in heaven; and it is conformity
to the same will that makes the ordinary actions of men on
earth become an acceptable service unto God.

The whole nature of virtue consists in conforming to the will
of God and the whole nature of vice is declining from the will

of God. All God's creatures are created to fulfill his will; the sun and the moon obey his will by the necessity of their nature; angels conform to his will by the perfection of their nature. If, therefore, you would show yourself not to be a rebel from the order of the creation, you must act like beings both above and below you. It must be the great desire of your soul that God's will may be done by you on earth as it is done in heaven. It must be the settled purpose and intention of your heart to will nothing, design nothing, do nothing, but in so far as you have reason to believe that it is the will of God that you should so desire, design, and do.

You are therefore to consider yourself as a being that has no other business in the world but to be that which God requires you to be. You are to have no rules of your own, to seek no self-designs or self-ends, but to fill some place and act some part in strict conformity and thankful resignation to the divine pleasure. Such resignation to the divine will signifies a cheerful approbation and thankful acceptance of everything that comes from God. It is not enough patiently to submit, but we must thankfully receive and fully approve of everything that by the order of God's providence happens to us.

Now this is our true state with relation to God. We cannot be said so much as to believe in him unless we believe him to be of infinite wisdom. Every argument, therefore, for patience under his disposal of us is as strong an argument for approbation and thankfulness for everything that he does to us. And there needs no more to dispose us to this gratitude toward God than a full belief in him that he is this Being of infinite wisdom, love, and goodness. Do but assent to this truth in the same manner as you assent to things of which you have no doubt, and then you will cheerfully approve of everything that

God has already approved for you.

Whenever, therefore, you find yourself disposed to uneasiness, or murmuring at anything that is the effect of God's providence over us, you must look upon yourself as denying either the wisdom or the goodness of God. For every complaint necessarily supposes this. You would never complain of your neighbor but that you suppose you can show either his unwise, unjust, or unkind behavior toward you. Now every murmuring, impatient reflection under the providence of God is the same accusation of God. A complaint always supposes ill usage.

This resignation to the divine will may be considered in two respects: first, as it signifies a thankful approbation of God's general providence over the world; secondly, as it signifies a thankful acceptance of his particular providence over us.

First, every man is, by the law of his creation, by the first article of his creed, obliged to consent to and acknowledge the wisdom and goodness of God in his general providence over the whole world. He is to believe that it is the effect of God's great wisdom and goodness that the world itself was formed at such a particular time and in such a manner; that the general order of nature, the whole frame of things, is contrived and formed in the best manner. He is to believe that God's providence over states and kingdoms, times and seasons, is all for the best: that the revolutions of state and changes of empire, the rise and fall of monarchies, persecutions, wars, famines, and plagues are all permitted and conducted by God's providence to the general good of man in this state of trial. A good man is to believe all this, with the same fullness of assent as he believes that God is in every place, though he neither sees nor can comprehend the manner of his presence.

When we think of God himself we are to have no sentiments

but of praise and thanksgiving. Even so, when we look at those things which are under the direction of God and governed by his providence, we are to receive them with the same attitudes of praise and gratitude. And though we are not to think all things right and just and lawful that the providence of God permits — for then nothing could be unjust because nothing is without his permission — yet we must adore God in the greatest public calamities and the most grievous persecutions, as things that are permitted by God for ends suitable to his wisdom and glory in the government of the world.

There is nothing more suitable to the piety of a reasonable creature or to the spirit of a Christian than thus to approve, admire, and glorify God in all the acts of his general providence — considering the whole world as his particular family and all events as directed by his wisdom. For if the Christian cannot thank and praise God as well in calamities and sufferings as in prosperity and happiness, he is as far from the piety of a Christian as that man is who only loves them that love him. For to thank God only for such things as you like is no more a proper act of piety than to believe only what you see is an act of faith. Resignation and thanksgiving to God are only acts of piety when they are acts of faith, trust, and confidence in the divine goodness.

Thus much concerning resignation to the divine will as it signifies a thankful approbation of God's general providence. It is now to be considered as it signifies a thankful acceptance of God's particular providence over us.

Every man is to consider himself as a particuar object of God's providence — under the same care and protection of God as if the world had been made for him alone. It is not by chance that any man is born at such a time, of such parents, and in such a place and condition. The Scriptures assure us that it was by divine appointment that our blessed Saviour was born at Bethlehem and at such a time. Now although it was owing to the dignity of his person and the great importance of his birth that thus much of the divine counsel was declared to the world, yet we are as sure, from the same Scriptures, that the time and manner of every man's coming into the world is according to some eternal purposes and direction of divine providence.

As it is thus certain that we are what we are as to birth, time, and condition of entering into the world since all that is particular in our state is the effect of God's particular providence over us and intended for some particular ends both of his glory and our own happiness, we are called upon to conform and resign our will to the will of God in all these respects, thankfully approving and accepting everything that is particular in our state. Had you been anything else than what you are, you would have been, all things considered, less wisely provided for than you are now. You would have lacked some circumstances and conditions that are best fitted to make you happy and serviceable to the glory of God.

Could you see all that God sees, all that happy chain of causes and motives which are to move and invite you to a right course of life, you would see something to make you like that state you are in as better for you than any other. But since you cannot see this, your Christian faith and trust in God is to exercise itself and render you as grateful and thankful for the happiness of your state as if you saw everything that contributes to it with your own eyes.

But now if this is the case of every man in the world, thus blessed with some particular state that is most convenient for him, how reasonable is it for every man to will that which

God has already willed for him! And by a pious faith and trust in the divine goodness, thankfully to adore and magnify that wise providence which he is sure has made the best choice for him of those things which he could not choose for himself!

It is just thus in the various conditions of life. If you give yourself up to uneasiness or complain at anything in your state, you may, for aught you know, murmur at that very thing which is to prove the cause of your salvation. Had you the power to get that which you think it is so grievous to lack, it might perhaps be that very thing which would most expose you to eternal damnation.

So whether we consider the infinite goodness of God that cannot choose amiss for us, or our own great ignorance of what is most advantageous to us, there can be nothing so reasonable and pious as to have no will but that of God's — to desire nothing for ourselves, in our persons, our state, and condition, but that which the good providence of God appoints us.

If we are right in believing God to act over us with infinite wisdom and goodness, then we cannot carry our notions of conformity and resignation to the divine will too high. Neither can we ever be deceived by thinking that to be best for us which God has brought upon us. For the providence of God is not more concerned in the government of night and day and the variety of seasons than in the common course of events that seem most to depend upon the mere wills of men. It is as strictly right, therefore, to look upon all worldly accidents and changes, all the various turns and alternations in your own life, to be as truly the effects of divine providence as the rising and setting of the sun or the alternations of the seasons of the year. As you are always to adore the wisdom of God in the direction of these things, so it is the same reasonable duty always to magnify God as an equal Director of everything that happens to you in the course of your own life.

Since this holy resignation and conformity of your will to the will of God is so much the true state of piety, I hope you will think it proper to make this hour of prayer a constant season of applying to God for so great a gift. By thus constantly praying for it your heart may be habitually disposed toward it and always in a state of readiness to look at everything as God's. There is nothing that so powerfully governs the heart, that so strongly excites us to wise reasonable actions, as a true sense of God's presence. But we cannot see or apprehend the essence of God so much as this holy resignation which attributes everything to him and receives everything as from him.

Now you must not reserve the exercise of this attitude to any particular times or occasions, or fancy how resigned you will be to God if such or such trials should happen. This is amusing yourself with the notion or idea of resignation instead of the virtue itself. Do not, therefore, please yourself with thinking how you would act and submit to God in a plague, or famine, or persecution, but rather be intent upon the perfection of the present day. And be assured that the best way of showing a true zeal is to make little things the occasions of great piety.

Begin therefore in the smallest matters and most ordinary occasions, and accustom your mind to the daily exercise of this frame of mind in the lowest occurrences of life. And when a contempt, an affront, a little injury, or the smallest disappointments of every day continually raise your mind to God in proper acts of resignation, then you may justly hope that you shall be numbered among those who are resigned and thankful to God in the greatest trials and afflictions.

Chapter XXIII

The Necessity and Nature of Confession

I AM NOW come to six o'clock in the evening which, according to the Scripture account, is called the twelfth or last
hour of the day. This is a time so proper for devotion that I
suppose nothing need be said to recommend it as a season of
prayer to all people who profess any regard to piety.

As the labor and action of life is generally over at this hour,
this is the proper time for everyone to call himself to account
and review all his behavior from the first action of the day.
The necessity of this examination is founded upon the necessity of repentance. For if it be necessary to repent of all our
sins, if the guilt of unrepented sins still continue upon us, then
it is necessary that all our sins and the particular circumstances
and aggravations of them be known, recollected, and brought
to repentance.

The Scripture saith, "If we confess our sins, he is faithful
and just to forgive us our sins, and to cleanse us from all un-
righteousness." Which is as much as to say that our sins are
forgiven — and we cleansed from the guilt and unrighteous-
ness of them — only when they are thus confessed and repented
of. There seems therefore to be the greatest necessity that all
our daily actions be constantly observed and brought to account, lest by negligence we load ourselves with the guilt of
unrepented sins.

This examination of ourselves every evening is, therefore, to be considered as something that is as necessary as a daily confession and repentance of our sins. Daily repentance has very little significance and loses all its chief benefit, unless it be a particular confession and repentance of the sins of that day. This examination is necessary to repentance in the same manner time is necessary. You cannot repent or express your sorrow, unless you allow some time for it. Neither can you repent, except so far as you know what it is that you are repenting of. So when it is said that it is necessary to examine and call your actions to account, it is only saying that it is necessary to know what and how many things you are to repent of.

You perhaps have hitherto only been accustomed to confess yourself a sinner in general and ask forgiveness in the gross, without any particular remembrance or contrition for the particular sins of that day. And by this practice you are brought to believe that the same short general form of confession of sin in general is sufficient repentance for every day.

Suppose another person should hold that a confession of our sins in general once at the end of every week was sufficient; and that it was as well to confess the sins of seven days altogether as to have a particular repentance at the end of every day: I know you sufficiently see the unreasonableness and impiety of this opinion and that you think it is easy enough to show the danger and folly of it. Yet you cannot bring one argument against such an opinion but what will be as good an argument against such a daily repentance as does not call the particular sins of that day to a strict account. For if your own particular sins are left out of your confession, your confessing of sin in general has no more effect upon your mind than if you had only confessed that all men in general are sinners. And there is nothing in any confession to show that it is yours, but so far as it is a self-accusation, not of sin in general, or such as is common to all others, but of such particular sins as are your own proper shame and reproach.

To proceed: In order to make this examination still more beneficial, every man should oblige himself to a certain method in it. As every man has something particular in his nature, stronger inclinations to some vices than others, some infirmities that stick closer to him and are harder to be conquered than others — and as it is as easy for every man to know this of himself as to know whom he likes or dislikes — so it is highly necessary that these particularities of our natures and tempers should never escape a severe trial. Nothing but a rigorous severity against these natural tempers is sufficient to conquer them.

Ponder these great truths: that the Son of God was forced to become man, to be partaker of all our infirmities, to undergo a poor, painful, miserable, and contemptible life, to be persecuted, hated, and at last nailed to a cross, that by such sufferings he might render God propitious to that nature in which he suffered; that all the bloody sacrifices and atonements of the Jewish law were to represent the necessity of this great sacrifice, and the great displeasure God bore to sinners; that the world is still under the curse of sin and certain marks of God's displeasure at it, such as famines, plagues, tempests, sickness, diseases, and death.

Consider these great truths: that this mysterious redemption, all these sacrifices and sufferings, both of God and man, are only to remove the guilt of sin. Then let this teach you with what tears and contrition you ought to purge yourself from it.

After this general consideration of the guilt of sin which has done so much mischief to your nature and exposed it to so great punishment, and made it so odious to God that nothing less than so great an atonement of the Son of God, and so great repentance of our own, can restore us to the divine favor, consider next your own particular share in the guilt of sin. And if you would know with what zeal you ought to repent yourself, consider how you would exhort another sinner to repentance, and what repentance and amendment you would expect from him whom you judged to be the greatest sinner in the world:

First, because you know more of the folly of your own heart than you do of other people's, you can charge yourself with various sins that you only know of yourself and cannot be sure that other sinners are guilty of them. So that as you know more of the folly, the baseness, the pride, the deceitfulness and negligence of your own heart than you do of anyone's else, so you have just reason to consider yourself as the greatest sinner that you know — because you know more of the greatness of your own sins than you do of other people's.

Secondly, the greatness of our guilt arises chiefly from the greatness of God's goodness toward us, from the particular graces and blessings, the favors, the lights and instructions that we have received from him. Now as these graces and blessings and the multitude of God's favors toward us are the great aggravations of our sins against God, so they are known only to ourselves. Therefore, every sinner knows more of the aggravations of his own guilt than he does of other people's. Consequently, he may justly look upon himself to be the greatest sinner that he knows.

Lastly, to conclude this chapter: Having thus examined and confessed your sins at this hour of the evening, you must afterward look upon yourself as still obliged to betake yourself to prayer again just before you go to bed.

The subject that is most proper for your prayers at that time is death. Let your prayers, therefore, then be wholly upon it, reckoning upon all the dangers, uncertainties, and terrors of death. Let them contain everything that can affect and awaken your mind into just apprehensions of death. Let your petitions be all for right sentiments of the approach and importance of death. Beg of God that your mind may be possessed with such a sense of its nearness that you may have it always in your thoughts, do everything as in sight of it, and make every day a day of preparation for it.

Represent to your imagination that your bed is your grave; that all things are ready for your interment; that you are to have no more to do with this world; and that it will be owing to God's great mercy if you ever see the light of the sun again or have another day to add to your works of piety. Then commit yourself to sleep as one that is to have no more opportunities of doing good, but is to awake among spirits that are separate from the body and waiting for the judgment of the last great day.

Such a solemn resignation of yourself into the hands of God every evening, and parting with all the world as if you were never to see it any more — and all this in the silence and darkness of the night — is a practice that will soon have excellent effects upon your spirit. For this time of the night is exceeding proper for such prayers and meditations. The likeness which sleep and darkness have to death will contribute very much to make your thoughts about it the more deep and affecting. So that I hope you will not let a time so proper for such prayers be ever passed over without them.

CHAPTER XXIV

*The Excellency and Greatness
of a Devout Spirit*

I HAVE NOW FINISHED what I intended in this treatise. I have
explained the nature of devotion, both as it signifies a life
devoted to God and as it signifies a regular method of daily
prayer. I have now only to add a word or two in recommendation of a life governed by this spirit of devotion.

People of fine parts and learning may think it hard to have
their lack of devotion charged upon their ignorance. If, however, they will be content to be tried by reason and Scripture, it
will be made to appear that a lack of devotion — either among
the learned or unlearned — is founded in gross ignorance.

Who reckons it a sign of a poor or little mind for a man to
be full of reverence and duty to his parents, to have the truest
love and honor for his friend, or to excel in the highest instances of gratitude to his benefactor? Are not these attitudes
in the highest degree in the most exalted and perfect minds?
And yet what is high devotion but the highest exercise of these
same attitudes of duty, reverence, love, honor, and gratitude to
the amiable and glorious Parent, Friend, and Benefactor of all
mankind?

Further, that part of devotion which expresses itself in sor-
rowful confessions and penitential tears of a broken and contrite heart is very far from being any sign of a little and igno-

rant mind. Who does not acknowledge it an instance of an ingenuous, generous, and brave mind to acknowledge a fault and ask pardon for any offense? Are not the finest and most improved minds the most remarkable for this excellent trait? Is it not also agreed that the ingenuity and excellence of a man's spirit is much shown when his sorrow and indignation at himself rises in proportion to the folly of his crime and the goodness and greatness of the person he has offended?

Now if things are thus, then the greater any man's mind is, the more he knows of God and himself, the more will he be disposed to prostrate himself before God in all the humblest acts and expressions of repentance. The greater the ingenuity, the generosity, the judgment, and the penetration of his mind, the more will he exercise and indulge a passionate, tender sense of God's just displeasure. And the more he knows of the greatness, the goodness, and the perfection of the divine nature, the fuller of shame and confusion will he be at his own sins and ingratitude.

On the other hand, the more dull and ignorant any soul is, the more base and ungenerous it naturally is, the more senseless of the goodness and purity of God it is, so much the more averse will it be to all acts of humble confession and repentance.

Devotion, therefore, is so far from being best suited to little, ignorant minds that a true elevation of soul, a lively sense of honor, and a great knowledge of God and ourselves are the greatest natural helps for our devotion.

It shall now be made to appear by a variety of arguments that indevotion is founded on the most excessive ignorance.

First, our blessed Lord and his apostles were eminent instances of great and frequent devotion. Now if we will grant (as all Christians must grant) that their great devotion was founded in a true knowledge of the nature of devotion, the nature of God, and the nature of man — then it is plain that all those who are insensible of the duty of devotion know neither God nor themselves, nor devotion. For if a right knowledge in these three respects produces great devotion, as in the case of our Saviour and his apostles, then a neglect of devotion must be chargeable upon ignorance.

Again, how comes it that most people have recourse to devotion when they are in sickness, distress, or fear of death? Is it not because this state shows them more of the need of God and their own weakness than they perceive at other times? Is it not because their infirmities, their approaching end, convince them of something that they did not half perceive before? Now if devotion at these seasons is the effect of a better knowledge of God and ourselves, then the neglect of devotion at other times is always owing to great ignorance of God and ourselves.

Further, as indevotion is ignorance, so it is the most shameful ignorance and such as is to be charged with the greatest folly. This will fully appear to anyone who considers by what rules we are to judge of the excellency of any knowledge or the shamefulness of any ignorance. Now knowledge itself would be no excellence to us — nor ignorance any reproach — but that we are *rational* creatures. If there be any things that concern us more than others, if there be any truths that are more to us than all others, he who has the fullest knowledge of these things, who sees these truths in the clearest and strongest light, has the clearest understanding.

If, therefore, our relation to God be our greatest relation, if our advancement in his favor be our highest advancement, he who has the highest notions of the excellence of this relation, he who most strongly perceives the highest worth and great value of holiness and virtue, he who judges everything little when compared with it proves himself to be master of the best and most excellent knowledge.

If a judge has fine skill in painting, architecture, and music, but at the same time has gross and confused notions of equity and a poor, dull apprehension of the value of justice, who would scruple to reckon him a poor and ignorant judge? But if a judge is to be reckoned ignorant when he does not feel and perceive the value and worth of justice, then all common Christians are to be looked upon as more or less knowing accordingly as they know more or less of those great things which are the common and greatest concern of all Christians.

If a gentleman should fancy that the moon is no bigger than it appears to the eye, that it shines with its own light, that all the stars are only so many spots of light — and if, after reading books of astronomy, he should still continue in the same opinion — most people would think he had but a poor apprehension. But if the same person should think it better to provide for a short life here than to prepare for a glorious eternity hereafter, that it is better to be rich than to be eminent in piety, his ignorance and dullness would be too great to be compared to anything else.

There is no knowledge that deserves the name of it except that which we call judgment. All the rest is but the capacity of an animal. It is but mere seeing and hearing.

If a man had eyes that could see beyond the stars or pierce into the heart of the earth, but could not see the things that were before him or discern anything that was serviceable to him, we should reckon that he had very bad sight. If another had ears that received sounds from the world in the moon but could hear nothing that was said or done upon earth, we should look upon him to be as bad as deaf.

In like manner, if a man has a memory that can retain a great many things, if he has a wit that is sharp and acute in arts and sciences, or an imagination that can wander agreeably in fiction, but has a dull poor apprehension of his duty and relation to God, of the value of piety, or the worth of moral virtue, he may very justly be reckoned to have a bad understanding. He is like the man who can only see and hear such things as are of no benefit to him.

As the essence of stupidity consists in the entire lack of judgment, in an ignorance of the value of things, so the essence of wisdom and knowledge must consist in the excellency of our judgment or in the knowledge of the worth and value of things.

If, therefore, God be our greatest good — if there can be no good but in his favor, nor any evil but in departing from him — then it is plain that he who judges it the best thing he can do to please God to the utmost of his power, who worships and adores him with all his heart and soul, who would rather have a pious mind than all the dignities and honors in the world, shows himself to be in the highest state of human wisdom.

To proceed: We know how our blessed Lord acted in a human body. It was his meat and drink to do the will of his Father which is in heaven. And if any number of heavenly spirits were to leave their habitations in the light of God and be for a while united to human bodies, they would certainly tend toward God in all their actions and be as heavenly as they could in a state of flesh and blood.

All human spirits, therefore, the more exalted they are, the more they know their divine Original, the nearer they come to heavenly spirits — by so much the more will they live to God in all their actions, and make their whole life a state of devotion.

Devotion therefore is the greatest sign of a great and noble genius. It supposes a soul in its highest state of knowledge. None but little and blinded minds, sunk into ignorance and vanity, are destitute of it.

The greatest spirits of the heathen world, such as Pythagoras, Socrates, Plato, Epictetus, and Marcus Antoninus, owed all their greatness to the spirit of devotion. They were full of God. Their wisdom and deep contemplations tended only to deliver men from the vanity of the world and the slavery of bodily passions that they might act as spirits which had come from God and were soon to return to him.

Any devout man makes a true use of his reason. He sees through the vanity of the world, discovers the corruption of his nature, and admits the blindness of his passion. He lives by a law that is not visible to vulgar eyes; he sets eternity against time; and he chooses rather to be forever great in the presence of God than to have the greatest share of worldly pleasure while he lives.

He who is devout is full of these great thoughts. He lives upon these noble reflections, and conducts himself by rules and principles that can be apprehended, admired, and loved only by reason. There is nothing, therefore, that shows so great a genius, nothing that so plainly declares a heroic greatness of mind, as great devotion. When you suppose a man to be a saint you have raised him as much above all other conditions of life as a philosopher is above an animal.

Lastly, courage and bravery are words of a great sound and seem to signify a heroic spirit. Yet humility, which seems to be the lowest and meanest part of devotion, is a more certain argument for a noble and courageous mind. Humility contends with greater enemies, is more constantly engaged, more violently assaulted, bears more, suffers more, and requires greater courage to support itself than any instances of worldly bravery.

A man who dares be poor and contemptible in the eyes of the world to approve himself to God, who resists and rejects all human glory, who opposes the clamor of his passions, who meekly puts up with all injuries and wrongs and dares wait for his reward till the invisible hand of God gives to everyone his proper place, endures a much greater trial and exerts a nobler fortitude than he who is bold and daring in the fire of battle.

For the boldness of a soldier, if he is a stranger to the spirit of devotion, is rather weakness than fortitude. It is at best but mad passion and heated spirits. It has no more true valor in it than the fury of a tiger. For as we cannot lift up a hand or stir a foot but by a power that is lent us from God, so bold actions that are not directed by the laws of God are no more true bravery than sedate malice is Christian patience.

Reason is our universal law that obliges us in all places and at all times. No actions have any honor but so far as they are instances of our obedience to reason.

I have made this digression for the sake of those who think a great devotion to be bigotry and poorness of spirit. By these considerations they may see how poor all other tempers are when compared to it. They may see that all worldly attainments, whether of greatness, wisdom, or bravery, are but empty sounds. There is nothing wise or great or noble in a human spirit but rightly to know and heartily to worship and adore God — who is the support and life of all spirits, whether in heaven or on earth.

Printed in the United Kingdom
by Lightning Source UK Ltd.
102783UKS00001B/253-261